Understanding
Richard Wright's
Black Boy

The Greenwood Press "Literature in Context" Series

Understanding *To Kill a Mockingbird*: A Student Casebook to Issues, Sources, and Historical Documents
Claudia Durst Johnson

Understanding *The Scarlet Letter*: A Student Casebook to Issues, Sources, and Historical Documents
Claudia Durst Johnson

Understanding *Adventures of Huckleberry Finn*: A Student Casebook to Issues, Sources, and Historical Documents
Claudia Durst Johnson

Understanding *Macbeth*: A Student Casebook to Issues, Sources, and Historical Documents
Faith Nostbakken

Understanding *Of Mice and Men, The Red Pony*, and *The Pearl*: A Student Casebook to Issues, Sources, and Historical Documents
Claudia Durst Johnson

Understanding Anne Frank's *The Diary of a Young Girl*: A Student Casebook to Issues, Sources, and Historical Documents
Hedda Rosner Kopf

Understanding *Pride and Prejudice*: A Student Casebook to Issues, Sources, and Historical Documents
Debra Teachman

Understanding *The Red Badge of Courage*: A Student Casebook to Issues, Sources, and Historical Documents
Claudia Durst Johnson

UNDERSTANDING
Richard Wright's
Black Boy

A STUDENT CASEBOOK TO ISSUES, SOURCES, AND HISTORICAL DOCUMENTS

Robert Felgar

The Greenwood Press
"Literature in Context" Series
Claudia Durst Johnson, Series Editor

GREENWOOD PRESS
Westport, Connecticut • London

Library of Congress Cataloging-in-Publication Data

Felgar, Robert, 1944–
    Understanding Richard Wright's Black boy : a student casebook to
issues, sources, and historical documents / Robert Felgar.
        p.   cm.—(The Greenwood Press "Literature in context"
    series, ISSN 1074–598X)
    Includes bibliographical references (p.   ) and index.
    ISBN 0–313–30221–9 (alk. paper)
    1. Afro-American youth.   2. Wright, Richard, 1908–1960. Black
boy—Sources.   3. Wright, Richard, 1908–1960—Childhood and youth—
Sources.   4. Afro-American authors—20th century—Biography—
History and criticism—Sources.   5. Afro-American youth—History—
Sources.   I. Title.   II. Series.
PS3545.R815Z6518   1998
813'.52—DC21   97–40853

British Library Cataloguing in Publication Data is available.

Library of Congress Catalog Card Number: 97–40853
ISBN: 0–313–30221–9
ISSN: 1074–598X

First published in 1998

Greenwood Press, 88 Post Road West, Westport, CT 06881
An imprint of Greenwood Publishing Group, Inc.

Printed in the United States of America

∞™

The paper used in this book complies with the
Permanent Paper Standard issued by the National
Information Standards Organization (Z39.48–1984).
P

Acknowledgments

I want to thank three colleagues for their valuable suggestions about documents for this book: Randall C. Davis, William J. Hug, and Steven J. Whitton.

Copyright Acknowledgments

To Cindy

Contents

Introduction

Black Boy, Richard Wright's fictionalized autobiography, is a major addition and challenge to the American autobiographical tradition. Numerous attempts to censor it when it was first published in 1945, in the intervening years, and in the 1990s are just one indication of how important it is, whether read in the expurgated 1945 edition or the uncensored 1991 version. (This casebook contextualizes either edition equally well.) *Black Boy* steps on so many toes, is so powerfully written, and bears the marks of so much racial and social struggle that it is not a book that can be ignored: it is at the center of American experience.

It deals largely with a question that the United States still seems unwilling to face: Why are some Americans, no matter how capable, resourceful, intelligent, and trustworthy, mistreated for no discernible reason other than that their skin is darker than that of some of their fellow citizens? In other words, how should a human being react to being treated as less than human for the most absurd of reasons? Wright makes it clear in *Black Boy* that societies will go to almost any length to maintain the status quo, regardless of how weak it is in the face of logic and analysis. That this is still true and may remain true indefinitely is just one reason *Black Boy* endures. It also has sustained its readers' interest because it is such a powerful record of why Richard Wright did not become Bigger

Thomas, the protagonist in Wright's most famous novel, *Native Son*. Had Bigger's creator not turned to the writing of such intensely realized books, he might have become like the character. If white Americans denied Wright his humanness, *Black Boy* establishes and clarifies it.

Black Boy is likely to remain of interest, regardless of whether the United States ever solves its racial problems, because it is such a compelling version of that favorite American tale, the Horatio Alger myth—the notion that even if one is born on the wrong side of the tracks, one can make it in America if one is persistent, frugal, and hardworking. Wright was all those things and did make it in a sense, although he spent the last thirteen years of his life (1947–1960) in Paris.

Because the only kind of reading is reading between the lines, and because a lot of what readers need to read between the lines of *Black Boy* is not readily available, this volume serves the useful purpose of putting Wright's autobiography in the political, social, racial, literary, and general cultural contexts of when he lived and wrote. Even the most factual texts are not self-interpreting: they need context to make sense and to be appreciated. Although *Black Boy* can be read as a self-referential entity, it makes frequent gestures toward the world it interprets, especially the Deep South in the first third of the twentieth century, a world that has by no means completely disappeared, but one that is not as sharp-edged as it used to be.

Black Boy can be read largely in terms of literary form, as it is in the first chapter of this book. However, it is understood and enjoyed much more if the environment that it grew out of is re-created, which is what the rest of this casebook offers to do. By reprinting sources from many different areas—literature, history, the law, personal memories, anthropology, and recent editorials—this book makes the world that Wright experienced available again.

The documents reproduced here raise important questions about *Black Boy*:

- How can the literary form and themes of Wright's autobiography be viewed independently of all other considerations?
- How truthfully does *Black Boy* reflect the realities of life for African Americans in the South in the first third of the twentieth century?

• How much does Wright owe to the American autobiographical tradition? How does he depart from that tradition?

• How successful was Wright in dealing with the lies and absurd beliefs about black people he had to face?

• Is Wright overly negative toward his own community in *Black Boy*?

• How impressive is Wright's literary and personal achievement in *Black Boy*, given what the documents in this collection suggest he was up against?

A number of different kinds of sources are used to contextualize *Black Boy*:

• other autobiographies
• legal documents
• a novel
• an interview
• an anthropological study
• magazine articles
• a Congressional speech
• contemporary editorials

All these source materials help us understand how Wright's literary imagination worked in *Black Boy*: he shaped what the world gave him into an epic tale of his liberation from racial despair.

In addition to the documents, each chapter includes introductory discussions, study questions, topics for written or oral consideration, and a list of suggested readings.

Richard Wright. Photo reproduced from the collections of the Library of Congress.

1 ———————————————————

Literary Analysis: Dominant Themes and Structure of *Black Boy*

DOMINANT THEMES

Black Boy is informed by a number of basic ideas that preside over it: defiance of authority; physical and emotional violence; the author's consuming curiosity, hunger (for food, knowledge, life, and affection); religion as a means of social control; race; and literacy. As an unusually strong-willed individual, Richard Wright demonstrates repeatedly in *Black Boy* that authority should be based on truth rather than on tradition or power. The description of Wright setting fire to his grandparents' house makes it clear to the reader that even at the age of four the author is determined to find out what he can challenge successfully. He wants to know what authority is based on and why he should accept it. Realizing, for instance, that he cannot hope to challenge his father directly and prevail, Wright intentionally takes his father's words about killing a kitten literally in order to defy his authority by a willful misunderstanding. Similarly, he is determined to deliver the junior high school graduation speech he had written rather than the one the principal wanted him to give. According to Michel Fabre, Wright's most important biographer, the principal wanted to avoid any risk of offending whites, who were going to let him start a high school for black students. The same stiff resistance to authority lies behind

Wright's admiration for H. L. Mencken, who loved to mock God and authority, and behind the frequent difficulties he had with the Communist Party, which set itself up as an ultimate authority.

The violence in *Black Boy*, whether physical or otherwise, is extremely important, because it is what authority tends to rely on instead of argument. As Wright believed that arguments must succeed based on their own merits rather than on appeals to authority or violence, the reader can easily determine what Wright thinks of a world that is so quick to rely on force to meet challenges to it. After setting the house on fire, Wright is lashed so hard and so long that he passes out. His mother, grandmother, grandfather, Aunt Addie, and other relatives frequently beat him, slap him, and lash him. His Uncle Hoskins is killed by whites who envy his lucrative saloon business. Wright himself pulls a long bread knife on his Aunt Addie to protect himself from her, fights with other boys, and threatens his Uncle Tom with razor blades. Behind all these specific examples of the theme of physical violence lies the threat of lynching: violence is everywhere in *Black Boy*. Words, too, are frequently used to inflict pain, and the book itself may be viewed as a verbal assault on the world Wright grew up in.

Another dominant theme in *Black Boy* is hunger—hunger for food, life, love, knowledge, opportunity. In fact, the last third of the original manuscript was published in 1977, under the title *American Hunger*. Wright was frequently hungry in the most basic sense: often his family did not have enough food. Even by the late 1920s (he was born in 1908), he had to gorge himself to gain enough weight to be eligible for a job in the post office. He hated his father in part because he saw him as a competitor for food. When his mother took him to a kitchen where she cooked for a white family, Wright could see and smell the food, but except for occasional scraps, he was not allowed to eat it. Many times he was so weak from hunger that he could not do yard work at the orphanage where his mother was forced to leave him and his brother. At another time, he was so hungry that he almost sold his poodle to buy food.

Along with this kind of hunger, Wright also had an uncontrollable hunger for language and stories: when he hears the story *Bluebeard and His Seven Wives* for the first time, he is ecstatic; he is determined to hear or read more. In some moods, the secular young Wright was so starved for social interaction that he attended church just to satisfy the craving. He also felt a deep hunger for affection, especially from his mother, that was never satisfied. But what Wright hungered for most was life itself, as well as the chance to understand it without fearing violence or rejection. Being denied those two things was unbearable. Wright had an appetite for more options than his environment provided; it offered a ninth-grade formal education, libraries restricted to white patronage, a generally inferior (from Wright's point of view) community, severely limited job opportunities, and violent racism. But Wright's hunger could not be contained by these constraints.

A third major thematic concern in *Black Boy* is Wright's view of religion, in his case several versions of black Protestant Christianity, as social control. Wright was a one-worlder, that is to say, he thought that there was one world, and we are in it, so any notion of some "other" world was offensive to his intellectual sensibility. After he killed the kitten, his mother made him repeat after her a prayer in which Wright asks God to spare his life even though he did not spare the kitten's. Wright views the incident as an example of how religion uses terror to enforce norms that the community finds acceptable. In *Black Boy* religion translates as a form of violence and threat by other means. So strongly does Wright feel about the unethicalness of religion that he devotes almost all of chapter 4 to this theme. He felt the emotional appeal of religion, but, as he puts it, he had enough sense to see a doctor if he saw an angel. In Wright's view, the use of religion in the household of his grandmother, a Seventh-Day Adventist (one who believes that Saturday should be the day of worship and that Christ's second coming to the earth and the Last Judgment will occur soon), was unethical; even his mother's long illness was sometimes blamed on his faithlessness. At one point in chapter 4, a neighborhood boy, sent by his parents, asks Wright whether he is "saved," in an attempt to pressure Wright into conformity. Wright believed that there was very little that religious institutions would stop at in order to gain converts. Nevertheless, he also understood the function of religion—namely, to make up for what reality lacks—but he was implacably realistic. He also understood religion to be another form of power: when his mother encouraged him to join a Methodist church, she put her request in a form that was hard to resist: she said that if he loved her, he would join her church.

A fourth theme is race and racism. Wright dramatizes repeatedly the utter absurdity of basing "superiority" on skin color and of having to act inferior to satisfy the social and emotional needs of light-skinned people. As a child, Wright realized that race was an extremely dubious concept, particularly in light of the fact that his grandmother was as white as any "white" person. He never saw any evidence that race was a legitimate source of authority, but he was excluded by a society that assumed unthinkingly that it was. Taking on faith the humanity of other *men*, Wright could never really fathom why they could not do the same (they had too much to lose). Most of the book turns on the fundamental illogicality in white thinking that a person's value depends to a considerable extent on one's racial affiliation. Wright makes an overwhelming case that building social distinctions on racism is hopeless, no matter how elaborate the efforts to deny that fact.

Literacy is the fifth theme in his autobiography. As a child, Wright learned the power of written language by scribbling four-letter words on windows, which horrified his mother but nevertheless demonstrated to him that writing is a way of gaining some leverage on the world. Once, when he became bored while praying in his room, he wrote a story about an unhappy Indian girl who drowned herself. It was extremely gratifying to Wright that a young woman who lived next door was puzzled by his having written a story for no apparent reason. He also loved to read the cheap pulp tales that were printed in the newspaper he sold, until he learned that the paper was an organ of the Ku Klux Klan; but the tales themselves pointed toward a larger world, one of seductive and imaginative possibilities. Written language was Wright's salvation; it was a kind of secular religion for him. He was always careful, though, to distance himself from black English, which he seemed to view as a sign of inferiority. Writing was so important to him that it is not an exaggeration to say that it was equivalent to his sense of who he was, of his manhood. That is why he refused to work for a white woman who scoffed at his proclamation that he wanted to be a writer. Reading, too, was crucial in Wright's development: in Memphis he began reading the *Commercial Appeal, Harper's Magazine*, the *Atlantic Monthly*, and the *American Mercury*, all of which helped to feed his hungry mind, as did the many novels he devoured. After he went to Chicago and joined the Communist Party, he encountered another threat to his integrity as a writer:

the Party tried to tell him how to write. Wright's self-achieved literacy alarmed Party members.

STRUCTURE

To convey these themes to the reader, Wright uses a number of literary elements: (1) symbols, metaphors, and imagery, (2) point of view, (3) plot, (4) character, (5) setting, and (6) tone. Perhaps the most dominant symbol in *Black Boy*, hovering over so many pages of the book, even after Wright goes to Chicago, is the South. It represents an irrational force that can kill or maim at any time, that is based strictly on the whims of whites, and that must be escaped if Wright is to become a successful writer. Another symbol that figures prominently in Wright's narrative is books, which come to stand for possibility, opportunity, even life itself; more than for most other booklovers, books for Wright had a nearly magical quality, for they allowed him to visit worlds he was otherwise excluded from. A third symbol, the North, suggested escape and hope to Wright and to many other African Americans in the 1920s. The quietest symbol in *Black Boy* is Wright's mother, who was paralyzed by a stroke and bedridden as a result for years: she stands for the meaningless suffering Wright experienced and saw so much of; what she represents is really what so much of the book is about, but it is too painful for Wright to speak of her directly and at length.

Point of view and handling of language are other key literary conventions that Wright uses to convey his core ideas to the reader. The first-person narrator is in a tricky position, because he is looking back at the past (Wright calls *Black Boy* "a record of childhood and youth," but it is in fact fictionalized) and reporting and interpreting what the character Richard Wright experienced. The point of view is further complicated by the fact that the narrator bears witness to his own innocence, naïveté, and trustworthiness; this is a very difficult task, for the reader may wonder whether one can be self-aware and yet remain innocent. The narrator may also be guilty of "stair wit," that is, wit that originates as one is going down the stairs, *after* an event is over. For instance, the reader may wonder if Wright was really so innocent of the meaning of his words when he told Granny to kiss back there, meaning his buttocks. What is indisputable about the point of view, though, is that it reveals a hypersensitive young black man recalling the world that helped to make him what he was: anxious, very bright, lyrical, determined, ambitious, proud, suspicious. But he is also a narrator who describes the physical appearance of practically every woman the young Wright met, who represents his younger self as being almost the only sensitive and intelligent young black man in Mississippi, and who may have misremembered or rearranged some events. Even though the narrator reports his own virtue, and even though he may have other shortcomings, he nevertheless convinces us of the general trustworthiness of his account and of the value of the themes he is committed to.

The narrator's language varies greatly in syntax, diction, and tone. He is concerned, though, that the reader understand that he does not *write* black English, although his younger self sometimes speaks it. Wright often tends to use language as a weapon to attack injustice or racism, but he also uses it to render experiences and ideas as convincingly as possible. He wants his readers to trust him and to agree with him that he is a victim of an unjust, racist social system, but also to know that there is a lyrical side to his sensibility. That is why he sometimes pauses to describe natural beauty. One reason *Black Boy* is often regarded as Wright's best book is because his language here is at its best—flexible, resonant, powerful, an instrument deftly conveying the basic ideas of his autobiography.

The plot unfolds chronologically for the most part. The unexpurgated version of *Black Boy* is divided into two parts. "Southern Night" covers the years 1908–1927; "The Horror and the Glory" extends from 1927 to May Day 1936. The year 1927 is the linchpin because that was when Wright went to Chicago, although psychologically and emotionally he never left the South. *Black Boy* begins with the description of how he set fire to his grandparents' house and the severe beating he received as punishment. Early on we also learn that one reason the narrator despises his father is because the latter eats too much, while the young Richard Wright frequently goes hungry. Wright's father abandoned his wife and two sons for another woman, leaving the family in desperate straits. The narrator recounts an episode in which his mother would not let him back into the house until he stood up to a gang of boys who kept stealing the family grocery money. On the one hand, the plot makes it clear that the narrator was largely on his own in the world, that he could not afford to trust anyone but himself. He spends time in a saloon, watches what people do in outhouses, learns what goes on in whorehouses; his childhood is unlike that of the stereotypical middle-class American boy. On the other hand, Wright did have friends, did go to school, did have some semblance of a family life, and did learn to read, write, and count. The plot demonstrates that Wright was more a part of the black community than he may have wanted to admit: he heard gospel singing, he listened to black folktales, he spoke black English, he played the dozens (a game of verbal wit in which the goal is to insult one's antagonist's mother without losing one's own temper when the insults go the other way). He also had many different jobs and moved frequently with his family. As he grew older, he worked mainly because he wanted to be part of the Great Migration of black southerners to the North. In 1925 he finally made his way to Memphis, where he stayed with a Mrs. Moss and her daughter, Bess. In Memphis he also was maneuvered into fighting another young black man named Harrison for the amusement of whites, and he began reading and writing in earnest.

Part Two begins with Wright's arrival in Chicago, where he worked for a while at a restaurant that had a cook who spat in the food. In Chicago he also joined the Communist Party because it seemed to provide the emotional support he needed, as well as an intellectual framework to account for the experience of African Americans. He worked as a postal clerk, a janitor in a hospital, and a secretary for the John Reed Club (a Communist literary organization). Part Two discusses at some length political intrigue in the Communist Party—alleged conspiracies, plots, and suspicion exasperated and frightened the idealistic young Richard Wright, which is one reason he eventually left the party; the other reason was his intense dislike of its trying to tell him how to write. He also worked for the Federal Experimental Theater and the Federal Writers' Project during the Great Depression.

The highly episodic plot of the autobiography, with its action set in various towns in the South and in two northern cities—Chicago and New York—reflects a life of rapid and awkward transition from a southern, preindustrial mode of life to a northern, more urban, industrial one. The plot is structured to dramatize the developing consciousness of the man who came to write *Native Son* and *Black Boy*.

The characters reinforce Wright's dominant ideas in *Black Boy*. The most important characters are the narrator and the version of his younger self revealed in the autobiography. As narrator Wright can be characterized as apprehensive about gaining his readers' trust and as determined to set the world straight about his younger self and the world that surrounded him. The narrator is a relentless attacker of racism and groundless authority; he sees his experiences as overwhelming evidence for the basic callousness of the world to humane values. As smart, sensitive, curious, and imaginative as the narrator is, though, he is himself sometimes indifferent to black and white women and to blacks he regards as socially inferior. Keenly sensitive to the shortcomings of others, the narrator is blind to most of his own. His younger self, the hero of *Black Boy*, is a remarkable person who is determined, no matter what the odds, to realize his dream of becoming a writer and of living a truly human life. As necessary as his pride and strong will may have been, the protagonist possibly does not give the other characters enough credit.

Many of the minor characters are the narrator's relatives. His brother is a shadowy figure who rarely appears after the beginning episodes. He seems to have figured very little in Wright's consciousness. His father, however, is an object of strong hostility because Wright blames him for abandoning the family and for the family's state of continual hunger; he is what Wright does not want to be. Wright's mother seems to have done the best she could for her firstborn son, but from his point of view, it was not enough. Largely because of her poor health, Mrs. Wright was not able to give Richard the emotional support he wanted, and so he tries to repress both his deep ambivalence toward her and his anxiety about her affection for him. As a former schoolteacher, she encouraged Wright in his efforts to learn to read; but she was too beaten down by her husband's abandonment, her lack of money, the responsibility of rearing two boys, and particularly her poor health to be the mother Wright craved, and so he withdrew from her emotionally.

Wright seems to have been rather fond of one of his mother's sisters, Aunt Maggie, but his real favorite among his relatives, although they fought constantly, was his mother's mother, whose strict Seventh-Day Adventism was anathema to him. Granny believed she had a monopoly on religious truth and was not willing to negotiate the issue, but Wright rebelled against her insistence that he attend her church and not work on Saturday. She also disapproved of his reading and his writing. However, the two were much more alike than either would have wanted to admit, especially in their strong wills. It was only when her grandson threatened to leave her home, where he was living at the time, that she let him work on Saturday. After the protagonist himself, she is the most formidable character in the book. Her husband seems to have spent most of his time in a haze of bitterness over having been denied the federal pension he should have received as a Union veteran.

Among the numerous minor characters that function to support Wright's themes, Aunt Addie stands out. As a new teacher at a Seventh-Day Adventist school Wright attends, she is uncertain how she should act toward her nephew: when he refuses to tell her who has been eating walnuts in her classroom, she punishes him. The hostility between them grows until finally Wright threatens her with a knife in his grandmother's house, where she has tried to beat him again. Other notable minor characters include Griggs, a boyhood friend of Wright's who tries to tell him how whites expect him to act; Reynolds and Pease, who drive him away from his job at an optical company; Mrs. Moss and her daughter Bess, who befriend Wright in Memphis; Shorty, an elevator operator who allows whites to kick him in return for money; Harrison, who agrees to box with Wright for the amusement of a white audience; Mr. Falk, a white man who lends Wright his library card so he can check books out; the Finnish cook Tillie, who spits in the food; and Brand and Cooke, two men who work with Wright at a hospital in Chicago.

The setting of *Black Boy* is another means by which the author conveys his central ideas to his readers. To be born black in Mississippi in 1908, as Wright was, was to face the foreclosure of many of life's possibilities unless one was unusually resourceful and determined. African Americans could not vote or hold public office, attend white schools, marry whites, enjoy freedom of speech, or live anywhere they chose to. Black Americans also had to contend with segregated restaurants, public bathrooms, buses, trains, and drinking fountains; no white morticians would embalm a black corpse. The First World War (1914–1918) and the Great Depression (1929–1939) were defining events of the period. Most important, from Wright's point of view, it was a time when very few whites realized that blacks were every bit as human as they were. Part One is set in various towns in the South—Natchez, Mississippi; West Helena, Arkansas; Jackson, Mississippi; Memphis, Tennessee. It is what these places represent in *Black Boy*, though, that matters: a state of mind in the white community that tells blacks they are nothing; the South is more a mental environment than a physical place in Wright's autobiography. It is a white attitude that blacks must reject if they are to avoid its domination.

The tone of *Black Boy* ranges from the sarcastic to the lyrical to the indignant to the matter of fact. When the narrator refers to the love that binds his grandmother's house together, he is being bitterly sarcastic, because her home is based on physical and emotional abuse. The narrator is nevertheless keenly aware of the physical beauty of other human beings and of nature, which he describes lyrically. Confronted with the injustice and cruelty of so much of his environment, the narrator becomes outraged and indignant. In other words, the tone of *Black Boy* changes to meet its thematic demands.

Black Boy, then, is Richard Wright's very shrewdly and carefully crafted fictionalized autobiography. Its main purpose is to attack and refute the white South's view of him as a "boy," as an inferior version of whites. Sometimes loudly, sometimes quietly, Wright instructs his readers that they do not see him, but rather a belief about him. He is resolutely insisting, through the structure and themes of *Black Boy*, that he be granted the same dignity and autonomy his readers want for themselves. He is also looking for the understanding and sympathy that he felt lacking from his family, community, and the white South.

STUDY QUESTIONS

1. How much do you trust the narrator? Do you find him self-pitying? Worried that you will not believe him? In each case, justify your response.

2. Do you think the narrator gives enough credit to other black men? black women? white women? Why or why not?

3. *Black Boy* is subtitled "A Record of Childhood and Youth," but Wright's most important biographer, Michel Fabre, has documented factual inaccuracies in the book. For example, Wright did not quit his job at the first optical company because of Reynolds and Pease but in order to return to school in the fall; and the principal who wanted to look at his graduation speech was concerned about not offending whites, who were going to let him start a high school for black students. What differences do such factual inaccuracies make in the way you evaluate Wright's autobiography?

4. There may be a falling off of intensity in Part Two. If this is so, how would you account for it?

5. Why was Wright so attracted to the Communist Party? Why did the relationship not last?

6. How was Wright able to triumph over a system designed to crush him and all other African Americans?

7. What do you admire least and most about the narrator?

8. There is evidence that Wright was not as alienated from the black community as he makes out. How would you account for his possible exaggeration?

9. How successful is the author in solving the very difficult literary problem of using a first-person narrator who conveys how virtuous he is?

10. How tolerant would you say the narrator is of ethical and religious differences in others?

11. Does the narrator seem to understand the political, economic, and social importance of the black church?

TOPICS FOR WRITTEN OR ORAL EXPLORATION

1. Analyze the narrator and the character Richard Wright. What differences and similarities do you notice?

2. Write a short paper explaining why the young Richard Wright was even willing to try magic to gain some leverage on the world (see the list of magical possibilities toward the end of chapter 2).

3. In one of the most famous (or notorious) parts of *Black Boy*, near the beginning of chapter 2, the narrator expresses some alarming doubts about the black community. Write a paper in which you defend or attack the idea that the narrator sees the world through white eyes.

4. Is *Black Boy* too negative and pessimistic? Discuss.

5. If Wright's environment was virtually hopeless, how did it manage to produce him?

6. Write a paper explaining why the young Richard Wright would not learn his "place."

7. Discuss why Wright tried to burn down the house he was living in.

8. How would you account for the amount and the quality of the violence within and outside of the Wright family?

9. Why were the whites so unwilling to relinquish a system, racism, that could not possibly be justified? Discuss.

10. Does the episode about Wright almost selling his poodle misfire? Why or why not?

11. Write a paper explaining the narrator's attitude toward black women.

12. How sensitive is Wright to social class? How would you account for this?

13. Does Wright tend to look *at*, or *with*, other people?

14. Wright sometimes speaks black English, but as the narrator does not write that way. Why?

15. Michel Fabre says that Wright was not as restrained with Bess Moss as he claims. Explain the change in the facts.

16. Why was reading so important to Wright? Why did he particularly like realistic and naturalistic novels?

17. Contrast the expurgated 1945 edition of *Black Boy* with the unexpurgated 1991 edition. Would you say the 1991 edition is necessarily better? What changes were made, and why?

SUGGESTED READINGS

The following novels and autobiographies interact with *Black Boy* in revealing ways; some of them challenge Wright's perspective, whereas others extend it:

Angelou, Maya. *I Know Why the Caged Bird Sings*. New York: Random House, 1996.

Baldwin, James. *Go Tell It on the Mountain*. New York: Random House, 1995.

Cleaver, Eldridge. *Soul on Ice*. New York: Dell, 1970.

Crane, Stephen. *Maggie: A Girl of the Streets*. New York: Bantam Books, 1986.

Douglass, Frederick. *Narrative of the Life of Frederick Douglass*. New York: St. Martin's Press, 1993.

Ellison, Ralph. *Invisible Man*. New York: Random House, 1995.

Franklin, Benjamin. *Autobiography*. New York: Random House, 1990.

Jacobs, Harriet. *Incidents in the Life of a Slave Girl*. Edited by Jean Fagan Yellin. Cambridge, Mass.: Harvard University Press, 1987.

Twain, Mark. *The Adventures of Huckleberry Finn*. Berkeley: University of California Press, 1988.

Washington, Booker T. *Up from Slavery*. Edited by William L. Andrews. New York: Oxford University Press, 1995.

The following works include substantial sections on *Black Boy*:

Bloom, Harold, ed. *Richard Wright: Modern Critical Views*. New York: Chelsea House, 1987.

Fabre, Michel. *The Unfinished Quest of Richard Wright*. 2nd ed. Urbana: University of Illinois Press, 1993.

————. *The World of Richard Wright*. Jackson: University Press of Mississippi, 1985.

Felgar, Robert. *Richard Wright*. Boston: Twayne, 1980.

Gates, Henry Louis, Jr., and K. A. Appiah, eds. *Richard Wright: Critical Perspectives Past and Present*. New York: Amistad Press, 1993.

Kinnamon, Keneth. *The Emergence of Richard Wright*. Urbana: University of Illinois Press, 1972.

Macksey, Richard, and Frank E. Moorer, eds. *Richard Wright: A Collection of Critical Essays*. Englewood Cliffs, N.J.: Prentice-Hall, 1984.

Reilly, John M., ed. *Richard Wright: The Critical Reception*. New York: Franklin, 1978.

Walker, Margaret. *Richard Wright: Daemonic Genius*. New York: Warner, 1988.

2

The Autobiographical Tradition

Black Boy occupies a secure and important place in an old and ongoing literary tradition that can be traced back to St. Augustine's *Confessions*. From the early black autobiographies of Frederick Douglass and Booker T. Washington to the more recent examples of Claude Brown's *Manchild in the Promised Land* (1965) and *The Autobiography of Malcolm X* (1965), black American autobiography has called attention to the plight of the black person in white America. Unlike nineteenth-century black chroniclers, Wright did not have to overcome doubts about his authorship. The complete title of Douglass's first autobiography is *Narrative of the Life of Frederick Douglass, an American Slave, Written by Himself*; the complete title of Harriet Jacobs's autobiography is *Incidents in the Life of a Slave Girl, Written by Herself* (1861). Not even the hyperracist Senator Theodore Bilbo of Mississippi challenged Wright's authorship of *Black Boy*.

Less easily overcome was the powerful insistence in American autobiography that everyone should climb the ladder of "success." Ben Franklin made a very persuasive eighteenth-century case that in America a resourceful person can get ahead, even if there are formidable obstacles in one's path. He used his own life as evidence of the truth of this proposition. Frederick Douglass, too, saw his life as an ascent, particularly a movement north, out of slavery.

And Booker T. Washington proclaimed in *Up from Slavery* (1901) that slavery had been a "school" for African Americans from which they could emerge stronger and more enlightened, that is, more like him. W.E.B. Du Bois, in *The Souls of Black Folk* (1903), a book with autobiographical elements, was less optimistic about the likelihood of upward mobility for black people in America. Wright, writing several decades later, is motivated more by the Franklinian ideology than he realized.

In one particularly striking way, though, *Black Boy* diverges widely from the autobiographical tradition: Wright does not portray himself as a model for his readers to emulate; his way of living is his way of living. Unlike Franklin, Douglass, or Washington, Wright is not trying to show other people the way; he is describing only his way. This is what I have done, Wright declares; you are on your own. Such determined individualism is not to all tastes, but it is one of Wright's most salient features. Wright's cry is one of individual protest.

Like his male forebears in the autobiographical tradition, Wright is very much governed by gender-based assumptions. Women are not absent in *Black Boy*, but except for Wright's mother and grandmother, they are not taken very seriously, either. Since Homer, the dominant pattern of Western male experience has been the individual hero asserting himself against a hostile world: Wright seems at home in this mode in *Black Boy*. He confronts obstacle after obstacle alone: religion, his family, racism, poverty, other men, self-doubt. He relies on other men's books, but seldom other men. The heroic young protagonist in Wright's autobiography is imagined as self-sufficient, strong, and resourceful; he does not need the support of others. But this apparent self-reliance must be seen in context. Had Wright been, for instance, in Harriet Jacobs's circumstances as depicted in *Incidents in the Life of a Slave Girl*—a slave with two children—his ability to act heroically would have been severely limited. This is not to criticize Wright's personal achievement, but to clarify it.

THE SELF-MADE MAN

Often regarded as the archetypal American autobiography, Benjamin Franklin's life history early established that in the United States, life was based on unlimited upward mobility, providing that one was hardworking and driven to succeed. There are more parallels between Franklin's story and Wright's than one might expect: both were voracious readers, both spent time in France (Wright lived in France from 1947 until his death in 1960), both were extremely resourceful and determined, both were determined to escape oppression, both got ahead and made money, both were writers. The decisive difference, of course, was that one was black, the other white.

Although the selections reprinted here are from an edition that was published in 1909, the original edition was written from 1771–1790, and published in 1868.

FROM BENJAMIN FRANKLIN, *THE AUTOBIOGRAPHY* (1909)

Having emerged from the poverty and obscurity in which I was born and bred, to a state of affluence and some degree of reputation in the world, and having gone so far through life with a considerable share of felicity, the conducing means I made use of, which with the blessing of God so well succeeded, my posterity may like to know, as they may find some of them suitable to their own situations, and therefore fit to be imitated.

That felicity, when I reflected on it, has induced me sometimes to say, that were it offered to my choice, I should have no objection to a repetition of the same life from its beginning, only asking the advantages authors have in a second edition to correct some faults of the first. So I might, besides correcting the faults, change some sinister accidents and events of it for others more favorable. But though this were denied, I should still accept the offer. Since such a repetition is not to be expected, the next thing most like living one's life over again seems to be a recollection of that life, and to make that recollection as durable as possible by putting it down in writing.

Hereby, too, I shall indulge the inclination so natural in old men, to be talking of themselves and their own, past actions; and I shall indulge it without being tiresome to others, who, through respect to age, might conceive themselves obliged to give me a hearing, since this may be read or not as any one pleases. And, lastly (I may as well confess it, since my denial of it will be believed by nobody), perhaps I shall a good deal gratify my own *vanity*. Indeed, I scarce ever heard or saw the introductory words, *"Without vanity I may say,"* &c., but some vain thing immediately followed. Most people dislike vanity in others, whatever share they have of it themselves; but I give it fair quarter wherever I meet with it, being persuaded that it is often productive of good to the possessor, and to others that are within his sphere of action; and therefore, in many cases, it would not be altogether absurd if a man were to thank God for his vanity among the other comforts of life.

And now I speak of thanking God, I desire with all humility to acknowledge that I owe the mentioned happiness of my past life to His kind providence, which led me to the means I used and gave them success. My belief of this induces me to *hope*, though I must not *presume*, that the same goodness will still be exercised toward me, in continuing that happiness, or enabling me to bear a fatal reverse, which I may experience as others have done: the complexion of my future fortune being known to Him only in whose power it is to bless to us even our afflictions.

• • •

From a child I was fond of reading, and all the little money that came into my hands was ever laid out in books. Pleased with the Pilgrim's Progress, my first collection was of John Bunyan's works in separate little volumes. I afterward sold them to enable me to buy R. Burton's Historical Collections; they were small chapmen's books, and cheap, 40 or 50 in all. My father's little library consisted chiefly of books in polemic divinity, most of which I read, and have since often regretted that, at a time when I had such a thirst for knowledge, more proper books had not fallen in my way, since it was now resolved I should not be a clergyman. Plutarch's Lives there was in which I read abundantly, and I still think that time spent to great advantage. There was also a book of Da Foe's, called an Essay on Projects, and another of Dr. Mather's, called Essays to do Good, which perhaps gave me a turn of thinking that had an influence on some of the principal future events of my life.

This bookish inclination at length determined my father to make me a printer, though he had already one son (James) of the profession. In 1717 my brother James returned from England with a press and letters to set up his business in Boston. I liked it much better than that of my father, but still had a hankering for the sea. To prevent the apprehended effect of such an inclination, my father was impatient to have me bound to my brother. I stood out some time, but at last was persuaded, and signed the indentures when I was yet but twelve years old. I was to serve as an apprentice till I was twenty-one years of age, only I was to be allowed journeyman's wages during the last year. In a little time I made great proficiency in the business, and became a useful hand to my brother. I now had access to better books. An acquaintance with the apprentices of booksellers enabled me sometimes to borrow a small one, which I was careful to return soon and clean. Often I sat up in my room reading the greatest part of the night, when the book was borrowed in the evening and to be returned early in the morning, lest it should be missed or wanted.

And after some time an ingenious tradesman, Mr. Matthew Adams, who had a pretty collection of books, and who frequented our printing-house, took notice of me, invited me to his library, and very kindly lent me such books as I chose to read. I now took a fancy to poetry, and made some little pieces; my brother, thinking it might turn to account, encouraged me, and put me on composing occasional ballads. One was called *The Lighthouse Tragedy*, and contained an account of the drowning of Captain Worthilake, with his two daughters: the other was a sailor's song, on the taking of *Teach* (or Blackbeard) the pirate. They were wretched stuff, in the Grub-street-ballad style; and when they were printed he sent me about the town to sell them. The first sold wonderfully, the event being recent, having made a great noise. This flattered my vanity; but my father discouraged me by ridiculing my performances, and telling me verse-makers were generally beggars. So I escaped being a poet, most probably a very bad one; but as prose writing has been of great use to me in the course of my life, and was a principal means of my advancement, I shall tell you how, in such a situation, I acquired what little ability I have in that way.

• • •

My parents had early given me religious impressions, and brought me through my childhood piously in the Dissenting way. But I was scarce fifteen, when, after doubting by turns of several points, as I found them disputed in the different books I read, I began to doubt of Revelation itself. Some books against Deism fell into my hands; they were said to be the substance of sermons preached at Boyle's Lectures. It happened that they wrought an effect on me quite contrary to what was intended by them; for the arguments of the Deists, which were quoted to be re-futed, appeared to me much stronger than the refutations; in short, I soon became a thorough Deist. My arguments perverted some others, particularly Collins and Ralph; but, each of them having afterwards wrong'd me greatly without the least compunction, and recollecting

Keith's conduct towards me (who was another freethinker), and my own towards Vernon and Miss Read, which at times gave me great trouble, I began to suspect that this doctrine, tho' it might be true, was not very useful. My London pamphlet, which had for its motto these lines of Dryden:

> Whatever is, is right. Though purblind man
> Sees but a part o' the chain, the nearest link:
> His eyes not carrying to the equal beam,
> That poises all above;

and from the attributes of God, his infinite wisdom, goodness and power, concluded that nothing could possibly be wrong in the world, and that vice and virtue were empty distinctions, no such things existing, appear'd now not so clever a performance as I once thought it; and I doubted whether some error had not insinuated itself unperceiv'd into my argument, so as to infect all that follow'd, as is common in metaphysical reasonings.

• • •

[Here Franklin quotes a letter from Benjamin Vaughan, an admirer:] I would say to him, Sir, I solicit the history of your life from the following motives: Your history is so remarkable, that if you do not give it, somebody else will certainly give it; and perhaps so as nearly to do as much harm, as your own management of the thing might do good. It will moreover present a table of the internal circumstances of your country, which will very much tend to invite to it settlers of virtuous and manly minds. And considering the eagerness with which such information is sought by them, and the extent of your reputation, I do not know of a more efficacious advertisement than your biography would give. All that has happened to you is also connected with the detail of the manners and situation of a rising people; and in this respect I do not think that the writings of Caesar and Tacitus can be more interesting to a true judge of human nature and society. But these, sir, are small reasons, in my opinion, compared with the chance which your life will give for the forming of future great men; and in conjunction with your Art of Virtue (which you design to publish) of improving the features of private character, and consequently of aiding all happiness, both public and domestic. The two works I allude to, sir, will in particular give a noble rule and example of self-education. School and other education constantly proceed upon false principles, and show a clumsy apparatus pointed at a false mark; but your apparatus is simple, and the mark a true one; and while parents and young persons are left destitute of other just means of estimating and becoming prepared for a reasonable course in life, your discovery that the thing is in many a man's private power, will be invaluable! Influence upon the private character, late in life, is not only an influence late in life, but a weak influence. It is in youth that we plant our chief habits and prejudices; it is in youth that we take our party as to profession, pursuits and matrimony. In youth, therefore, the turn is given; in youth the education even of the next generation is given; in youth the private and public character is determined; and the term of life extending but from youth to age, life ought to begin well from youth, and more especially before we take our party as to our principal objects. But your biography will not merely teach self-education, but the education of a wise man; and the wisest man will receive lights and improve his progress, by seeing detailed the conduct of another wise man. And why are weaker men to be deprived of such helps, when we see our race has been blundering on in the dark, almost without a guide in this particular, from the farthest trace of time? Show then, sir, how much is to be done, both to sons and fathers; and invite all wise men to become like yourself, and other men to become wise. When we see how cruel statesmen and warriors can be to the human race, and how absurd distinguished men can be to their acquaintance, it will be instructive to observe the instances multiply of pacific, acquiescing manners; and to find how compatible it is to be great and domestic, enviable and yet good-humored.

New York: P. F. Collier and Son.

KINDRED SPIRITS

Wright was born just thirteen years after Frederick Douglass died in 1895. As this selection from Douglass's first version of his autobiography makes clear, both men believed deeply in the crucial importance of literacy, seeing it as a means of gaining freedom. Both were also determined to escape the oppressive conditions they were in, in Douglass's case slavery and in Wright's the near equivalent of it. And both were even willing to try magic as an aid against white hostility. The two men also shared the realization that they had to fight back or be crushed (Wright's fight with Aunt Maggie recalls Douglass's confrontation with the overseer Mr. Covey).

Chapter 6 is set in Baltimore, where Douglass had been taken in 1825 or 1826, when he was 7 or 8, to work for Hugh Auld and his wife; Auld was the brother of Douglass's former master's son-in-law, Thomas Auld. Also set in Baltimore, Chapter 7 covers the years 1825–1832, when Douglass would have been 7–14. Chapter 10 is set on the farm of one Mr. Covey, a slavebreaker to whom Douglass was sent in January 1, 1833, when he was 14. Mr. Covey's farm was 7 miles from St. Michael's, a town in Maryland where Thomas Auld, Douglass's master at the time, lived.

FROM FREDERICK DOUGLASS, *NARRATIVE OF THE LIFE OF FREDERICK DOUGLASS* (1845)

Chapter 6

My new mistress proved to be all she appeared when I first met her at the door,—a woman of the kindest heart and finest feelings. She had never had a slave under her control previously to myself, and prior to her marriage she had been dependent upon her own industry for a living. She was by trade a weaver; and by constant application to her business, she had been in a good degree preserved from the blighting and dehumanizing effects of slavery. I was utterly astonished at her goodness. I scarcely knew how to behave towards her. She was entirely unlike any other white woman I had ever seen. I could not approach her as I was accustomed to approach other white ladies. My early instruction was all out of place. The crouching servility, usually so acceptable a quality in a slave, did not answer when manifested toward her. Her favor was not gained by it; she seemed to be disturbed by it. She did not deem it impudent or unmannerly for a slave to look her in the face. The meanest slave was put fully at ease in her presence, and none left without feeling better for having seen her. Her face was made of heavenly smiles, and her voice of tranquil music.

But, alas! this kind heart had but a short time to remain such. The fatal poison of irresponsible power was already in her hands, and soon commenced its infernal work. That cheerful eye, under the influence of slavery, soon became red with rage; that voice, made all of sweet accord, changed to one of harsh and horrid discord; and that angelic face gave place to that of a demon.

Very soon after I went to live with Mr. and Mrs. Auld [his new master and mistress], she very kindly commenced to teach me the A, B, C. After I had learned this, she assisted me in learning to spell words of three or four letters. Just at this point of my progress, Mr. Auld found out what was going on, and at once forbade Mrs. Auld to instruct me further, telling her, among other things, that it was unlawful, as well as unsafe, to teach a slave to read. To use his own words, further, he said, "If you give a nigger an inch, he will take an ell. A nigger should know nothing but to obey his master—to do as he is told to do. Learning would *spoil* the best nigger in the world. Now," said he, "if you teach that nigger (speaking of myself) how to read, there would be no keeping him. It would forever unfit him to be a slave. He would at once become unmanageable, and of no value to his master. As to himself, it could do him no good, but a great deal of harm. It would make him discontented and unhappy." These words sank deep into my heart, stirred up sentiments within that lay slumbering, and called into existence an entirely new train of thought. It was a new and special revelation, explaining dark and mysterious things, with which my youthful understanding had struggled, but struggled in vain. I now understood what had been to me a most perplexing difficulty—to wit, the white man's power to enslave the black man. It was a grand achievement, and I prized it highly. From that moment, I understood the pathway from slavery to freedom. It was just what I wanted, and I got it at a time when I the least expected it. Whilst I was saddened by the thought of losing the aid of my kind mistress, I was gladdened by the invaluable instruction which, by the merest accident, I had gained from my master. Though conscious of the difficulty of learning without a teacher, I set out with high hope, and a fixed purpose, at whatever cost of trouble, to learn how to read. The very decided manner with which he spoke, and strove to impress his wife with the evil consequences of giving me instruction, served to convince me that he was deeply sensible of the truths he was uttering. It gave me the best assurance that I might rely with the utmost confidence on the results which, he said, would flow from teaching me to read. What he most dreaded, that I most desired. What he most loved, that I most hated. That which to him was a great evil, to be carefully shunned, was to me a great good, to be diligently sought; and the argument which he so warmly urged, against my learning to read, only served to inspire me with a desire and determination to learn. In learning to read, I owe almost as much to the bitter opposition of my master, as to the kindly aid of my mistress. I acknowledge the benefit of both.

I had resided but a short time in Baltimore before I observed a marked difference, in the treatment of slaves, from that which I had witnessed in the country. A city slave is almost a freeman, compared with a slave on the plantation. He is much better fed and clothed, and enjoys privileges altogether unknown to the slave on the plantation. There is a vestige of decency, a sense of shame, that does much to curb and check those outbreaks of atrocious cruelty so commonly enacted upon the plantation. He is a desperate slaveholder, who will shock the humanity of his non-slaveholding neighbors with the cries of his lacerated slave. Few are willing to incur the odium attaching to the reputation of being a cruel master; and above all things, they would not be known as not giving a slave enough to eat. Every city slaveholder is anxious to have it known of him, that he feeds his slaves well; and it is due to them to say, that most of them do give their slaves enough to eat. There are, however, some painful exceptions to this rule. Directly opposite to us, on Philpot Street, lived Mr. Thomas Hamilton. He owned two slaves. Their names were Henrietta and Mary. Henrietta was about twenty-two years of age, Mary was about fourteen; and of all the mangled and emaciated creatures I ever looked upon, these two were the most so. His heart must be harder than stone, that could look upon these unmoved. The head, neck, and shoulders of Mary were literally cut to pieces. I have frequently felt her head, and found it nearly covered with festering sores, caused by the lash of her cruel mistress. I do not know that her master ever whipped her, but I have been an eye-witness to the cruelty of Mrs. Hamilton. I used to be in Mr. Hamilton's house nearly every day. Mrs. Hamilton used to sit in a large chair in the middle of the room, with a very heavy cowskin always by her side, and scarce an hour passed during the day but was marked by the blood of one of these slaves. The girls seldom passed her without her saying, "Move faster you *black gip!*"—continuing, "If you don't move faster, I'll move you!" Added to the cruel lashings to which these slaves were subjected, they were kept nearly half-starved. They seldom knew what it was to eat a full meal. I have seen Mary contending with the pigs for the offal thrown into the street. So much was Mary kicked and cut to pieces, that she was oftener called *"pecked"* than by her name.

Chapter 7

I lived in Master Hugh's family about seven years. During this time, I succeeded in learning to read and write. In accomplishing this, I was compelled to resort to various stratagems. I had no regular teacher. My mistress, who had kindly commenced to instruct me, had, in compliance with the advice and direction of her husband, not only ceased to instruct, but had set her face against my being instructed by any one else. It is due, however, to my mistress to say of her, that she did not adopt this course of treatment immediately. She at first lacked the depravity indispensable to shutting me up in mental darkness. It was at least necessary for her to have some training in the exercise of irresponsible power, to make her equal to the task of treating me as though I were a brute.

My mistress was, as I have said, a kind and tender-hearted woman; and in the simplicity of her soul she commenced, when I first went to live with her, to treat me as she supposed one human being ought to treat another. In entering upon the duties of a slaveholder, she did not seem to perceive that I sustained to her the relation of a mere chattel, and that for her to treat me as a human being was not only wrong, but dangerously so. Slavery proved as injurious to her as it did to me. When I went there, she was a pious, warm, and tender-hearted woman. There was no sorrow or suffering for which she had not a tear. She had bread for the hungry, clothes for the naked, and comfort for every mourner that came within her reach. Slavery soon proved its ability to divest her of these heavenly qualities. Under its influence, the tender heart became stone, and the lamblike disposition gave way to one of tiger-like fierceness. The first step in her downward course was in her ceasing to instruct me. She now commenced to practise her husband's precepts. She finally became even more violent in her opposition than her husband himself. She was not satisfied with simply doing as well as he had commanded; she seemed anxious to do better. Nothing seemed to make her more angry than to see me with a newspaper. She seemed to think that here lay the danger. I have had her rush at me with a face made all up of fury, and snatch from me a newspaper, in a manner that fully revealed her apprehension. She was an apt woman; and a little experience soon demonstrated, to her satisfaction, that education and slavery were incompatible with each other.

From this time I was most narrowly watched. If I was in a separate room any considerable length of time, I was sure to be suspected of having a book, and was at once called to give an account of myself. All this, however, was too late. The first step had been taken. Mistress, in teaching me the alphabet, had given me the *inch*, and no precaution could prevent me from taking the *ell*.

The plan which I adopted, and the only one by which I was most successful, was that of making friends of all the little white boys whom I met in the street. As many of these as I could, I converted into teachers. With their kindly aid, obtained at different times and in different places, I finally succeeded in learning to read. When I was sent on errands, I always took my book with me, and by doing one part of my errand quickly, I found time to get a lesson before my return. I used also to carry bread with me, enough of which was always in the house, and to which I was always welcome; for I was much better off in this regard than many of the poor white children in our neighborhood. This bread I used to bestow upon the hungry little urchins, who, in return, would give me that more valuable bread of knowledge. I am strongly tempted to give the names of two or three of those little boys, as a testimonial of the gratitude and affection I bear them; but prudence forbids;—not that it would injure me, but it might embarrass them; for it is almost an unpardonable offence to teach slaves to read in this Christian country. It is enough to say of the dear little fellows, that they lived on Philpot Street, very near Durgin and Bailey's ship-yard. I used to talk this matter of slavery over with them. I would sometimes say to them, I wished I could be as free as they would be when they got to be men. "You will be free as soon as you are twenty-one, *but I am a slave for life!* Have not I as good a right to be free as you have?" These words used to trouble them; they would express for me the liveliest sympathy, and console me with the hope that something would occur by which I might be free.

I was now about twelve years old, and the thought of being *a slave for life* began to bear heavily upon my heart. Just about this time, I got hold of a book entitled "The Columbian Orator." Every opportunity I got, I used to read this book. Among much of other interesting matter, I found in it a dialogue between a master and his slave. The slave was represented as having run away from his master three times. The dialogue represented the conversation which took place between them, when the slave was retaken the third time. In this dialogue, the whole argument in behalf of slavery was brought forward by the master, all of which was disposed of by the slave. The slave was made to say some very smart as well as impressive things in reply to his master—things which had the desired though unexpected effect; for the conversation resulted in the voluntary emancipation of the slave on the part of the master.

In the same book, I met with one of Sheridan's [eighteenth-century British writer] mighty speeches on and in behalf of Catholic emancipation. These were choice documents to me. I read them over and over again with unabated interest. They gave tongue to interesting thoughts of my own soul, which had frequently flashed through my mind, and died away for want of utterance. The moral which I gained from the dialogue was the power of truth over the conscience of even a slaveholder. What I got from Sheridan was a bold denunciation of slavery, and a powerful vindication of human rights. The reading of these documents enabled me to utter my thoughts, and to meet the arguments brought forward to sustain slavery; but while they relieved me of one difficulty, they brought on another even more painful than the one of which I was relieved. The more I read, the more I was led to abhor and detest my enslavers. I could regard them in no other light than a band of successful robbers, who had left their homes, and gone to Africa, and stolen us from our homes, and in a strange land reduced us to slavery. I loathed them as being the meanest as well as the most wicked of men. As I read and contemplated the subject, behold! that very discontentment which Master Hugh [Douglass's former master] had predicted would follow my learning to read had already come, to torment and sting my soul to unutterable anguish. As I writhed under it, I would at times feel that learning to read had been a curse rather than a blessing. It had given me a view of my wretched condition, without the remedy. It opened my eyes to the horrible pit, but to no ladder upon which to get out. In moments of agony, I envied my fellow-slaves for their stupidity. I have often wished myself a beast. I preferred the condition of the meanest reptile to my own. Any thing, no matter what, to get rid of thinking! It was this everlasting thinking of my condition that tormented me. There was no getting rid of it. It was pressed upon me by every object within sight or hearing, animate or inanimate. The silver trump of freedom had roused my soul to eternal wakefulness. Freedom now appeared, to disappear no more forever. It was heard in every sound, and seen in every thing. It was ever present to torment me with a sense of my wretched condition. I saw nothing without seeing it, I heard nothing without hearing it, and felt nothing without feeling it. It looked from every star, it smiled in every calm, breathed in every wind, and moved in every storm.

I often found myself regretting my own existence, and wishing myself dead; and but for the hope of being free, I have no doubt but that I should have killed myself, or done something for which I should have been killed. While in this state of mind, I was eager to hear any one speak of slavery. I was a ready listener. Every little while, I could hear something about the abolitionists. It was some time before I found what the word meant. It was always used in such connections as to make it an interesting word to me. If a slave ran away and succeeded in getting clear, or if a slave killed his master, set fire to a barn, or did any thing very wrong in the mind of a slaveholder, it was spoken of as the fruit of *abolition*. Hearing the word in this connection very often, I set about learning what it meant. The dictionary afforded me little or no help. I found it was "the act of abolishing;" but then I did not know what was to be abolished. Here I was perplexed. I did not dare to ask any one about its meaning, for I was satisfied that it was something they wanted me to know very little about. After a patient waiting, I got one of our city papers, containing an account of the number of petitions from the north, praying for the abolition of slavery in the District of Columbia, and of the slave trade between the States. From this time I understood the words *abolition* and *abolitionist*, and always drew near when that word was spoken, expecting to hear something of importance to myself and fellow-slaves. The light broke in upon me by degrees. I went one day down on the wharf of Mr. Waters; and seeing two Irishmen unloading a scow of stone, I went, unasked, and helped them. When we had finished, one of them came to me and asked me if I were a slave. I told him I was. He asked, "Are ye a slave for life?" I told him that I was. The good Irishman seemed to be deeply affected by the statement. He said to the other that it was a pity so fine a little fellow as myself should be a slave for life. He said it was a shame to hold me. They both advised me to run away to the north; that I should find friends there, and that I should be free. I pretended not to be interested in what they said, and treated them as if I did not understand them; for I feared they might be treacherous. White men have been known to encourage slaves to escape, and then, to get the reward, catch them and return them to their masters. I was afraid that these seemingly good men might use me so; but I nevertheless remembered their advice, and from that time I resolved to run away. I looked forward to a time at which it would be safe for me to escape. I was too young to think of doing so immediately; besides, I wished to learn how to write, as I might have occasion to write my own pass. I consoled myself with the hope that I should one day find a good chance. Meanwhile, I would learn to write.

The idea as to how I might learn to write was suggested to me by being in Durgin and Bailey's ship-yard, and frequently seeing the ship carpenters, after hewing, and getting a piece of timber ready for use, write on the timber the name of that part of the ship for which it was intended. When a piece of timber was intended for the larboard side, it would be marked thus—"L." When a piece was for the starboard side, it would be marked thus—"S." A piece for the larboard side forward, would be marked thus—"L. F." For larboard aft, it would be marked thus— "L. A.". . . For starboard aft, it would be marked thus—"S. A." I soon learned the names of these letters, and for what they were intended when placed upon a piece of timber in the ship-yard. I immediately commenced copying them, and in a short time was able to make the four letters named. After that, when I met with any boy who I knew could write, I would tell him I could write as well as he. The next word would be, "I don't believe you. Let me see you try it." I would then make the letters which I had been so fortunate as to learn, and ask him to beat that. In this way I got a good many lessons in writing, which it is quite possible I should never have gotten in any other way. During this time, my copy-book was the board fence, brick wall, and pavement; my pen and ink was a lump of chalk. With these, I learned mainly how to write. I then commenced and continued copying the Italics in Webster's Spelling Book, until I could make them all without looking on the book. By this time, my little Master Thomas [the son of Douglass's master] had gone to school, and learned how to write, and had written over a number of copy-books. These had been brought home, and shown to some of our near neighbors, and then laid aside. My mistress used to go to class meeting at the Wilk Street meetinghouse every Monday afternoon, and leave me to take care of the house. When left thus, I used to spend the time in writing in the spaces left in Master Thomas's copy-book, copying what he had written. I continued to do this until I could write a hand very similar to that of Master Thomas. Thus, after a long, tedious effort for years, I finally succeeded in learning how to write.

Chapter 10

After threatening me thus, he [Thomas Auld] gave me a very large dose of salts, telling me that I might remain in St. Michael's that night, (it being quite late,) but that I must be off back to Mr. Covey's early in the morning; and that if I did not, he would *get hold of me*, which meant that he would whip me. I remained all night, and, according to his orders, I started off to Covey's in the morning, (Saturday morning,) wearied in body and broken in spirit. I got no supper that night, or breakfast that morning. I reached Covey's about nine o'clock; and just as I was getting over the fence that divided Mrs. Kemp's fields from ours, out ran Covey with his cowskin, to give me another whipping. Before he could reach me, I succeeded in getting to the cornfield; and as the corn was very high, it afforded me the means of hiding. He seemed very angry, and searched for me a long time. My behavior was altogether unaccountable. He finally gave up the chase, thinking, I suppose, that I must come home for something to eat; he would give himself no further trouble in looking for me. I spent that day mostly in the woods, having the alternative before me,—to go home and be whipped to death, or stay in the woods and be starved to death. That night, I fell in with Sandy Jenkins, a slave with whom I was somewhat acquainted. Sandy had a free wife who lived about four miles from Mr. Covey's; and it being Saturday, he was on his way to see her. I told him my circumstances, and he very kindly invited me to go home with him. I went home with him, and talked this whole matter over, and got his advice as to what course it was best for me to pursue. I found Sandy an old adviser. He told me, with great solemnity, I must go back to Covey; but that before I went, I must go with him into another part of the woods, where there was a certain *root*, which, if I would take some of it with me, carrying it *always on my right side*, would render it impossible for Mr. Covey, or any other white man, to whip me. He said he had carried it for years; and since he had done so, he had never received a blow, and never expected to while he carried it. I at first rejected the idea, that the simple carrying of a root in my pocket would have any such effect as he had said, and was not disposed to take it; but Sandy impressed the necessity with much earnestness, telling me it could do no harm, if it did no good. To please him, I at length took the root, and, according to his direction, carried it upon my right side. This was Sunday morning. I immediately started for home; and upon entering the yard gate, out came Mr. Covey on his way to meeting. He spoke to me very kindly, bade me drive the pigs from a lot near by, and passed on towards the church. Now, this singular conduct of Mr. Covey really made me begin to think that there was something in the *root* which Sandy had given me; and had it been on any other day than Sunday, I could have attributed the conduct to no other cause than the influence of that root; and as it was, I was half inclined to think the *root* to be something more than I at first had taken it to be. All went well till Monday morning. On this morning the virtue of the *root* was fully tested. Long before daylight, I was called to go and rub, curry, and feed, the horses. I obeyed, and was glad to obey. But whilst thus engaged, whilst in the act of throwing down some blades from the loft, Mr. Covey entered the stable with a long rope, and just as I was half out of the loft, he caught hold of my legs, and was about tying me. As soon as I found what he was up to, I gave a sudden spring, and as I did so, he holding to my legs, I was brought sprawling on the stable floor. Mr. Covey seemed now to think he had me, and could do what he pleased; but at this moment—from whence came the spirit I don't know—I resolved to fight; and, suiting my action to the resolution, I seized Covey hard by the throat; and as I did so, I rose. He held on to me, and I to him. My resistance was so entirely unexpected, that Covey seemed taken all aback. He trembled like a leaf. This gave me assurance, and I held him uneasy, causing the blood to run where I touched him with the ends of my fingers. Mr. Covey soon called out to Hughes [another slave] for help. Hughes came, and while Covey held me, attempted to tie my right hand. While he was in the act of doing so, I watched my chance, and gave him a heavy kick close under the ribs.

This kick fairly sickened Hughes, so that he left me in the hands of Mr. Covey. This kick had the effect of not only weakening Hughes, but Covey also. When he saw Hughes bending over with pain, his courage quailed. He asked me if I meant to persist in my resistance. I told him I did, come what might; that he had used me like a brute for six months, and that I was determined to be used so no longer. With that, he strove to drag me to a stick that was lying just out of the stable door. He meant to knock me down. But just as he was leaning over to get the stick, I seized him with both hands by his collar, and brought him by a sudden snatch to the ground. By this time, Bill [another slave] came. Covey called upon him for assistance. Bill wanted to know what he could do. Covey said, "Take hold of him, take hold of him!" Bill said his master hired him out to work, and not help to whip me; so he left Covey and myself to fight our own battle out. We were at it for nearly two hours. Covey at length let me go, puffing and blowing at a great rate, saying that if I had not resisted, he would not have whipped me half so much. The truth was, that he had not whipped me at all. I considered him as getting entirely the worst end of the bargain; for he had drawn no blood from me, but I had from him. The whole six months afterwards, that I spent with Mr. Covey, he never laid the weight of his finger upon me in anger. He would occasionally say, he didn't want to get hold of me again. "No," thought I, "you need not; for you will come off worse than you did before."

This battle with Mr. Covey was the turning-point in my career as a slave. It rekindled the few expiring embers of freedom, and revived within me a sense of my own manhood. It recalled the departed self-confidence, and inspired me again with a determination to be free. The gratification afforded by the triumph was a full compensation for whatever else might follow, even death itself. He only can understand the deep satisfaction which I experienced, who has himself repelled by force the bloody arm of slavery. I felt as I never felt before. It was a glorious resurrection, from the tomb of slavery, to the heaven of freedom. My long-crushed spirit rose, cowardice departed, bold defiance took its place; and I now re-solved that, however long I might remain a slave in form, the day had passed forever when I could be a slave in fact. I did not hesitate to let it be known of me, that the white man who expected to succeed in whip-ping, must also succeed in killing me.

From this time I was never again what might be called fairly whipped, though I remained a slave four years afterwards. I had several fights, but was never whipped.

It was for a long time a matter of surprise to me why Mr. Covey did not immediately have me taken by the constable to the whipping-post, and there regularly whipped for the crime of raising my hand against a white man in defence of myself. And the only explanation I can now think of does not entirely satisfy me; but such as it is, I will give it. Mr. Covey enjoyed the most unbounded reputation for being a first-rate overseer and negro-breaker. It was of considerable importance to him. That reputation was at stake; and had he sent me—a boy about sixteen years old—to the public whipping-post, his reputation would have been lost; so, to save his reputation, he suffered me to go unpunished.

My term of actual service to Mr. Edward Covey ended on Christmas day, 1833. The days between Christmas and New Year's day are allowed as holidays; and, accordingly, we were not required to perform any labor, more than to feed and take care of the stock. This time we regarded as our own, by the grace of our masters; and we therefore used or abused it nearly as we pleased. . . .

• • •

The week before our intended start [escape from slavery], I wrote several protections, one for each of us. [Douglass planned to run away with his fellow slaves Henry Harris, John Harris, Henry Bailey, and Charles Roberts.] As well as I can remember, they were in the following words, to wit:—

> This is to certify that I, the undersigned, have given the bearer, my servant, full liberty to go to Baltimore, and spend the Easter holidays. Written with mine own hand, &c., 1835.
>
>   William Hamilton [the father-in-law of Douglass's master],
>   Near St. Michael's, in Talbot county, Maryland.

We were not going to Baltimore; but, in going up the bay, we went toward Baltimore, and these protections were only intended to protect us while on the bay.

As the time drew near for our departure, our anxiety became more and more intense. It was truly a matter of life and death with us. The strength of our determination was about to be fully tested. At this time, I was very active in explaining every difficulty, removing every doubt, dispelling every fear, and inspiring all with the firmness indispensable to success in our undertaking; assuring them that half was gained the instant we made the move; we had talked long enough; we were now ready to move; if not now, we never should be; and if we did not intend to move now, we had as well fold our arms, sit down, and acknowledge ourselves fit only to be slaves. This, none of us were prepared to acknowledge. Every man stood firm; and at our last meeting, we pledged ourselves afresh, in the most solemn manner, that, at the time appointed, we would certainly start in pursuit of freedom. This was in the middle of the week, at the end of which we were to be off. We went, as usual, to our several fields of labor, but with bosoms highly agitated with thoughts of our truly hazardous undertaking. We tried to conceal our feelings as much as possible; and I think we succeeded very well.

Boston: Anti-Slavery Society.

THE WIZARD OF TUSKEGEE

Wright was born seven years after the publication of Booker T. Washington's *Up from Slavery* (1901). The younger autobiographer could afford to be more candid than his predecessor because, while Washington was trying to accumulate power, money, and influence for himself and for Tuskegee Institute (later renamed Tuskegee University), Wright was bent on attacking a racist way of life in *Black Boy*. He was writing to express his own outrage, not to garner support for an institution. Where Wright comes in the front door, Washington comes, hat in hand, to the back door.

Nevertheless, Washington was probably the most powerful black American who has ever lived, whereas Wright never had much power. Washington was determined to acquire economic power for himself and other ex-slaves; political and social power could come later. He was not interested in literary power, the kind that attracted Wright, as the older man's inert, leaden prose reveals. Wright's lyrical and imaginative style would not have suited Washington, who wanted to be perceived as someone white philanthropists, politicians, and businessmen could trust. Washington presents himself as humble and simple, when in reality he was neither. The kind of pose revealed in Washington's statement that he must have been born somewhere and sometime would have disgusted Wright.

FROM BOOKER T. WASHINGTON, *UP FROM SLAVERY* (1901)

Chapter 1

A Slave Among Slaves

I was born a slave on a plantation in Franklin County, Virginia. I am not quite sure of the exact place or exact date of my birth, but at any rate I suspect I must have been born somewhere and at some time. As nearly as I have been able to learn, I was born near a cross-roads post-office called Hale's Ford, and the year was 1858 or 1859. I do not know the month or the day. The earliest impressions I can now recall are the plantation and the slave quarters—the latter being the part of the plantation where the slaves had their cabins.

My life had its beginning in the midst of the most miserable, desolate, and discouraging surroundings. This was so, however, not because my owners were especially cruel, for they were not, as compared with many others. I was born in a typical log cabin, about fourteen by sixteen feet square. In this cabin I lived with my mother and a brother and sister till after the Civil War, when we were all declared free.

Of my ancestry I know almost nothing. In the slave quarters, and even later, I heard whispered conversations among the coloured people of the tortures which the slaves, including, no doubt, my ancestors on my mother's side, suffered in the middle passage of the slave ship while being conveyed from Africa to America. I have been unsuccessful in securing any information that would throw any accurate light upon the history of my family beyond my mother. She, I remember, had a half-brother and a half-sister. In the days of slavery not very much attention was given to family history and family records—that is, black family records. My mother, I suppose, attracted the attention of a purchaser who was afterward my owner and hers. Her addition to the slave family attracted about as much attention as the purchase of a new horse or cow. Of my father I know even less than of my mother. I do not even know his name. I have heard reports to the effect that he was a white man who lived on one of the near-by plantations. Whoever he was, I never heard of his taking the least interest in me or providing in any way for my rearing. But I do not find especial fault with him. He was simply another unfortunate victim of the institution which the Nation unhappily had engrafted upon it at the time.

The cabin was not only our living-place, but was also used as the kitchen for the plantation. My mother was the plantation cook. The cabin was without glass windows; it had openings in the side which let in the light, and also the cold, chilly air of winter. There was a door to the cabin—that is, something that was called a door—but the uncertain hinges by which it was hung, and the large cracks in it, to say nothing of the fact that it was too small, made the room a very uncomfortable one. In addition to these openings there was, in the lower right hand corner of the room, the "cat-hole,"—a contrivance which almost every mansion or cabin in Virginia possessed during the antebellum period. The "cat-hole" was a square opening, about seven by eight inches, provided for the purpose of letting the cat pass in and out of the house at will during the night. In the case of our particular cabin I could never understand the necessity for this convenience, since there were at least a half-dozen other places in the cabin that would have accommodated the cats. There was no wooden floor in our cabin, the naked earth being used as a floor.

In the centre of the earthen floor there was a large, deep opening covered with boards, which was used as a place in which to store sweet potatoes during the winter. An impression of this potato-hole is very distinctly engraved upon my memory, because I recall that during the process of putting the potatoes in or taking them out I would often come into possession of one or two, which I roasted and thoroughly enjoyed. There was no cooking-stove on our plantation, and all the cooking for the whites and slaves my mother had to do over an open fireplace, mostly in pots and "skillets." While the poorly built cabin caused us to suffer with cold in the winter, the heat from the open fireplace in summer was equally trying.

The early years of my life, which were spent in the little cabin, were not very different from those of thousands of other slaves. My mother, of course, had little time in which to give attention to the training of her children during the day. She snatched a few moments for our care in the early morning before her work began, and at night after the day's work was done. One of my earliest recollections is that of my mother cooking a chicken late at night, and awakening her children for the purpose of feeding them. How or where she got it I do not know. I presume, however, it was procured from our owner's farm. Some people may call this theft. If such a thing were to happen now, I should condemn it as theft myself. But taking place at the time it did, and for the reason that it did, no one could ever make me believe that my mother was guilty of thieving. She was simply a victim of the system of slavery. I cannot remember having slept in a bed until after our family was declared free by the Emancipation Proclamation. Three children—John, my older brother, Amanda, my sister, and myself—had a pallet on the dirt floor, or, to be more correct, we slept in and on a bundle of filthy rags laid upon the dirt floor.

I was asked not long ago to tell something about the sports and pastimes that I engaged in during my youth. Until that question was asked it had never occurred to me that there was no period of my life that was devoted to play. From the time that I can remember anything, almost every day of my life has been occupied in some kind of labour; though I think I would now be a more useful man if I had had time for sports. During the period that I spent in slavery I was not large enough to be of much service, still I was occupied most of the time in cleaning the yards, carrying water to the men in the fields, or going to the mill, to which I used to take the corn, once a week, to be ground. The mill was about three miles from the plantation. This work I always dreaded. The heavy bag of corn would be thrown across the back of the horse, and the corn divided about evenly on each side; but in some way, almost without exception, on these trips, the corn would shift as to become unbalanced and would fall off the horse, and often I would fall with it. As I was not strong enough to reload the corn upon the horse, I would have to wait, sometimes for many hours, till a chance passer-by came along who would help me out of my trouble. The hours while waiting for some one were usually spent in crying. The time consumed in this way made me late in reaching the mill, and by the time I got my corn ground and reached home it would be far into the night. The road was a lonely one, and often led through dense forests. I was always frightened. The woods were said to be full of soldiers who had deserted from the army, and I had been told that the first thing a deserter did to a Negro boy when he found him alone was to cut off his ears. Besides, when I was late in getting home I knew I would always get a severe scolding or a flogging.

I had no schooling whatever while I was a slave, though I remember on several occasions I went as far as the schoolhouse door with one of my young mistresses to carry her books. The picture of several dozen boys and girls in a schoolroom engaged in study made a deep impression upon me, and I had the feeling that to get into a schoolhouse and study in this way would be about the same as getting into paradise.

So far as I can now recall, the first knowledge that I got of the fact that we were slaves, and that freedom of the slaves was being discussed, was early one morning before day, when I was awakened by my mother kneeling over her children and fervently praying that Lincoln and his armies might be successful, and that one day she and her children might be free. In this connection I have never been able to understand how the slaves throughout the South, completely ignorant as were the masses so far as books or newspapers were concerned, were able to keep themselves so accurately and completely informed about the great National questions that were agitating the country. From the time that Garrison, Lovejoy, and others began to agitate for freedom, the slaves throughout the South kept in close touch with the progress of the movement. Though I was a mere child during the preparation for the Civil War and during the war itself, I now recall the many late-at-night whispered discussions that I heard my mother and the other slaves on the plantation indulge in. These discussions showed that they understood the situation, and that they kept themselves informed of events by what was termed the "grape-vine" telegraph.

During the campaign when Lincoln was first a candidate for the Presidency, the slaves on our far-off plantation, miles from any railroad or large city or daily newspaper, knew what the issues involved were. When war was begun between the North and the South, every slave on our plantation felt and knew that, though other issues were discussed, the primal one was that of slavery. Even the most ignorant members of my race on the remote plantations felt in their hearts, with a certainty that admitted of no doubt, that the freedom of the slaves would be the one great result of the war, if the Northern armies conquered. Every success of the Federal armies and every defeat of the Confederate forces was watched with the keenest and most intense interest. Often the slaves got knowledge of the results of great battles before the white people received it. This news was usually gotten from the coloured man who was sent to the post-office for the mail. In our case the post-office was about three miles from the plantation and the mail came once or twice a week. The man who was sent to the office would linger about the place long enough to get the drift of the conversation from the group of white people who naturally congregated there, after receiving their mail, to discuss the latest news. The mail-carrier on his way back to our master's house would as naturally retail the news that he had secured among the slaves, and in this way they often heard of important events before the white people at the "big house," as the master's house was called.

I cannot remember a single instance during my childhood or early boyhood when our entire family sat down to the table together, and God's blessing was asked, and the family ate a meal in a civilized manner. On the plantation in Virginia, and even later, meals were gotten by the children very much as dumb animals get theirs. It was a piece of bread here and a scrap of meat there. It was a cup of milk at one time and some potatoes at another. Sometimes a portion of our family would eat out of the skillet or pot, while some one else would eat from a tin plate held on the knees, and often using nothing but the hands with which to hold the food. When I had grown to sufficient size, I was required to go to the "big house" at meal-times to fan the flies from the table by means of a large set of paper fans operated by a pulley. Naturally much of the conversation of the white people turned upon the subject of freedom and the war, and I absorbed a good deal of it. I remember that at one time I saw two of my young mistresses and some lady visitors eating ginger-cakes, in the yard. At that time those cakes seemed to me to be absolutely the most tempting and desirable things that I had ever seen; and I then and there resolved that, if I ever got free, the height of my ambition would be reached if I could get to the point where I could secure and eat ginger-cakes in the way that I saw those ladies doing.

Of course as the war was prolonged the white people, in many cases, often found it difficult to secure food for themselves. I think the slaves felt the deprivation less than the whites, because the usual diet for the slaves was corn bread and pork, and these could be raised on the plantation; but coffee, tea, sugar, and other articles which the whites had been accustomed to use could not be raised on the plantation, and the conditions brought about by the war frequently made it impossible to secure these things. The whites were often in great straits. Parched corn was used for coffee, and a kind of black molasses was used instead of sugar. Many times nothing was used to sweeten the so-called tea and coffee.

The first pair of shoes that I recall wearing were wooden ones. They had rough leather on the top, but the bottoms, which were about an inch thick, were of wood. When I walked they made a fearful noise, and besides this they were very inconvenient, since there was no yielding to the natural pressure of the foot. In wearing them one presented an exceedingly awkward appearance. The most trying ordeal that I was forced to endure as a slave boy, however, was the wearing of a flax shirt. In the portion of Virginia where I lived it was common to use flax as part of the clothing for the slaves. That part of the flax from which our clothing was made was largely the refuse, which of course was the cheapest and roughest part. I can scarcely imagine any torture, except, perhaps, the pulling of a tooth, that is equal to that caused by putting on a new flax shirt for the first time. It is almost equal to the feeling that one would experience if he had a dozen or more chestnut burrs, or a hundred small pin-points, in contact with his flesh. Even to this day I can recall accurately the tortures that I underwent when putting on one of these garments. The fact that my flesh was soft and tender added to the pain. But I had no choice. I had to wear the flax shirt or none; and had it been left to me to choose, I should have chosen to wear no covering. In connection with the flax shirt, my brother John, who is several years older than I am, performed one of the most generous acts that I ever heard of one slave relative doing for another. On several occasions when I was being forced to wear a new flax shirt, he generously agreed to put it on in my stead and wear it for several days, till it was "broken in." Until I had grown to be quite a youth this single garment was all that I wore.

One may get the idea from what I have said, that there was bitter feeling toward the white people on the part of my race, because of the fact that most of the white population was away fighting in a war which would result in keeping the Negro in slavery if the South was successful. In the case of the slaves on our place this was not true, and was not true of any large portion of the slave population in the South where the Negro was treated with anything like decency. During the Civil War one of my young masters was killed, and two were severely wounded. I recall the feeling of sorrow which existed among the slaves when they heard of the death of "Mars' Billy." It was no sham sorrow but real. Some of the slaves had nursed "Mars' Billy"; others had played with him when he was a child. "Mars' Billy" had begged for mercy in the case of others when the overseer or master was thrashing them. The sorrow in the slave quarter was only second to that in the "big house." When the two young masters were brought home wounded, the sympathy of the slaves was shown in many ways. They were just as anxious to assist in the nursing as the family relatives of the wounded. Some of the slaves would even beg for the privilege of sitting up at night to nurse their wounded masters. This tenderness and sympathy on the part of those held in bondage was a result of their kindly and generous nature. In order to defend and protect the women and children who were left on the plantations when the white males went to war, the slaves would have laid down their lives. The slave who was selected to sleep in the "big house" during the absence of the males was considered to have the place of honour. Any one attempting to harm "young Mistress" or "old Mistress" during the night would have had to cross the dead body of the slave to do so. I do not know how many have noticed it, but I think that it will be found to be true that there are few instances, either in slavery or freedom, in which a member of my race has been known to betray a specific trust.

As a rule, not only did the members of my race entertain no feelings of bitterness against the whites before and during the war, but there are many instances of Negroes tenderly caring for their former masters and mistresses who for some reason have become poor and dependent since the war. I know of instances where the former masters of slaves have for years been supplied with money by their former slaves to keep them from suffering. I have known of still other cases in which the former slaves have assisted in the education of the descendants of their former owners. I know of a case on a large plantation in the South in which a young white man, the son of the former owner of the estate, has become so reduced in purse and self-control by reason of drink that he is a pitiable creature; and yet, notwithstanding the poverty of the coloured people themselves on this plantation, they have for years supplied this young white man with the necessities of life. One sends him a little coffee or sugar, another a little meat, and so on. Nothing that the coloured people possess is too good for the son of "old Mars' Tom," who will perhaps never be permitted to suffer while any remain on the place who knew directly or indirectly of "old Mars' Tom."

I have said that there are few instances of a member of my race betraying a specific trust. One of the best illustrations of this which I know of is in the case of an ex-slave from Virginia whom I met not long ago in a little town in the state of Ohio. I found that this man had made a contract with his master, two or three years previous to the Emancipation Proclamation, to the effect that the slave was to be permitted to buy himself, by paying so much per year for his body; and while he was paying for himself, he was to be permitted to labour where and for whom he pleased. Finding that he could secure better wages in Ohio, he went there. When freedom came, he was still in debt to his master some three hundred dollars. Notwithstanding that the Emancipation Proclamation freed him from any obligation to his master, this black man walked the greater portion of the distance back to where his old master lived in Virginia, and placed the last dollar, with interest, in his hands. In talking to him about this, the man told me that he knew that he did not have to pay the debt, but that he had given his word to his master, and his word he had never broken. He felt that he could not enjoy his freedom till he had fulfilled his promise.

From some things that I have said one may get the idea that some of the slaves did not want freedom. This is not true. I have never seen one who did not want to be free, or one who would return to slavery.

I pity from the bottom of my heart any nation or body of people that is so unfortunate as to get entangled in the net of slavery. I have long since ceased to cherish any spirit of bitterness against the Southern white people on account of the enslavement of my race. No one section of our country was wholly responsible for its introduction, and, besides, it was recognized and protected for years by the General Government. Having once got its tentacles fastened on to the economic and social life of the Republic, it was no easy matter for the country to relieve itself of the institution. Then, when we rid ourselves of prejudice, or racial feeling, and look facts in the face, we must acknowledge that notwithstanding the cruelty and moral wrong of slavery, the ten million Negroes inhabiting this country, who themselves or whose ancestors went through the school of American slavery, are in a stronger and more hopeful condition, materially, intellectually, morally, and religiously, than is true of an equal number of black people in any other portion of the globe. This is so to such an extent that Negroes in this country, who themselves or whose forefathers went through the school of slavery, are constantly returning to Africa as missionaries to enlighten those who remained in the fatherland. This I say, not to justify slavery—on the other hand, I condemn it as an institution, as we all know that in America it was established for selfish and financial reasons, and not from a missionary motive—but to call attention to a fact, and to show how Providence so often uses men and institutions to accomplish a purpose. When persons ask me in these days how, in the midst of what sometimes seem hopelessly discouraging conditions, I can have such faith in the future of my race in this country, I remind them of the wilderness through which and out of which, a good Providence has already led us.

Ever since I have been old enough to think for myself, I have entertained the idea that, notwithstanding the cruel wrongs inflicted upon us, the black man got nearly as much out of slavery as the white man did. The hurtful influences of the institutions were not by any means confined to the Negro. This was fully illustrated by the life upon our own plantation. The whole machinery of slavery was so constructed as to cause labour, as a rule, to be looked upon as a badge of degradation, of inferiority. Hence labour was something that both races on the slave plantation sought to escape. The slave system on our place, in a large measure, took the spirit of self-reliance and self-help out of the white people. My old master had many boys and girls, but not one, so far as I know, ever mastered a single trade or special line of productive industry. The girls were not taught to cook, sew, or to take care of the house. All of this was left to the slaves. The slaves, of course, had little personal interest in the life of the plantation, and their ignorance prevented them from learning how to do things in the most improved and thorough manner. As a result of the system, fences were out of repair, gates were hanging half off the hinges, doors creaked, window-panes were out, plastering had fallen but was not replaced, weeds grew in the yard. As a rule, there was food for whites and blacks, but inside the house, and on the dining-room table, there was wanting that delicacy and refinement of touch and finish which can make a home the most convenient, comfortable, and attractive place in the world. Withal there was a waste of food and other materials which was sad. When freedom came, the slaves were almost as well fitted to begin life anew as the master, except in the matter of book-learning and ownership of property. The slave owner and his sons had mastered no special industry. They unconsciously had imbibed the feeling that manual labour was not the proper thing for them. On the other hand, the slaves, in many cases, had mastered some handicraft, and none were ashamed, and few unwilling, to labour.

Finally the war closed, and the day of freedom came. It was a momentous and eventful day to all upon our plantation. We had been expecting it. Freedom was in the air, and had been for months. Deserting soldiers returning to their homes were to be seen every day. Others who had been discharged, or whose regiments had been paroled, were constantly passing near our place. The "grape-vine telegraph" was kept busy night and day. The news and mutterings of great events were swiftly carried from one plantation to another. In the fear of "Yankee" invasions, the silverware and other valuables were taken from the "big house," buried in the woods, and guarded by trusted slaves. Woe be to any one who would have attempted to disturb the buried treasure. The slaves would give the Yankee soldiers food, drink, clothing—anything but that which had been specifically instrusted to their care and honour. As the great day drew nearer, there was more singing in the slave quarters than usual. It was bolder, had more ring, and lasted later into the night. Most of the verses of the plantation songs had some reference to freedom. True, they had sung those same verses before, but they had been careful to explain that the "freedom" in these songs referred to the next world, and had no connection with life in this world. Now they gradually threw off the mask, and were not afraid to let it be known that the "freedom" in their songs meant freedom of the body in this world. The night before the eventful day, word was sent to the slave quarters to the effect that something unusual was going to take place at the "big house" the next morning. There was little, if any, sleep that night. All was excitement and expectancy. Early the next morning word was sent to all the slaves, old and young, to gather at the house. In company with my mother, brother, and sister, and a large number of other slaves, I went to the master's house. All of our master's family were either standing or seated on the veranda of the house, where they could see what was to take place and hear what was said. There was a feeling of deep interest, or perhaps sadness, on their faces, but not bitterness. As I now recall the impression they made upon me, they did not at the moment seem to be sad because of the loss of property, but rather because of parting with those whom they had reared and who were in many ways very close to them. The most distinct thing that I now recall in connection with the scene was that some man who seemed to be a stranger (a United States officer, I presume) made a little speech and then read a rather long paper—the Emancipation Proclamation, I think. After the reading we were told that we were all free, and could go when and where we pleased. My mother, who was standing by my side, leaned over and kissed her children, while tears of joy ran down her cheeks. She explained to us what it all meant, that this was the day for which she had been so long praying, but fearing that she would never live to see.

For some minutes there was great rejoicing, and thanksgiving, and wild scenes of ecstasy. But there was no feeling of bitterness. In fact, there was pity among the slaves for our former owners. The wild rejoicing on the part of the emancipated coloured people lasted but for a brief period, for I noticed that by the time they returned to their cabins there was a change in their feelings. The great responsibility of being free, of having charge of themselves, of having to think and plan for themselves and their children, seemed to take possession of them. It was very much like suddenly turning a youth of ten or twelve years out into the world to provide for himself. In a few hours the great questions with which the Anglo-Saxon race had been grappling for centuries had been thrown upon these people to be solved. These were the questions of a home, a living, the rearing of children, education, citizenship, and the establishment and support of churches. Was it any wonder that within a few hours the wild rejoicing ceased and a feeling of deep gloom seemed to pervade the slave quarters? To some it seemed that, now that they were in actual possession of it, freedom was a more serious thing than they had expected to find it. Some of the slaves were seventy or eighty years old; their best days were gone. They had no strength with which to earn a living in a strange place and among strange people, even if they had been sure where to find a new place of abode. To this class the problem seemed especially hard. Besides, deep down in their hearts there was a strange and peculiar attachment to "old Marster" and "old Missus," and to their children, which they found it hard to think of breaking off. With these they had spent in some cases nearly a half-century, and it was no light thing to think of parting. Gradually, one by one, stealthily at first, the older slaves began to wander from the slave quarters back to the "big house" to have a whispered conversation with their former owners as to the future.

New York: Doubleday, Page and Co.

DOUBLE CONSCIOUSNESS

Two years after *Up from Slavery* was published, W.E.B. Du Bois published *The Souls of Black Folk*, partly as a challenge to Washington's autobiography. Du Bois's book, a combination of autobiography, history, sociology, economics, spirituals, and philosophy, countered Washington's emphasis on vocational education and economic development for black Americans with an emphasis on a liberal arts education and civil rights. Du Bois's book has been one of the most frequently cited works ever written by a black American. Every black intellectual in this century has had to react to it. Du Bois was involved in the founding of the National Association for the Advancement of Colored People, and he kept a close eye on racial developments in the United States until he died in 1963, by which time he was so thoroughly disillusioned by the country's racial prospects that he had moved to Ghana.

The Souls of Black Folk contains in its first chapter its most influential concept, an idea that resonates throughout *Black Boy*: the double consciousness of African Americans, a people who are and are not Americans. If freedom is at the core of any definition of "American," then no one is more American than that group that has been pursuing freedom for four hundred years; but no group has met with more obstacles in the pursuit of freedom. One of the great ironies of American history has been to describe people like Douglass, Wright, and Malcolm X as dangerous radicals, when they have been so insistent in wanting for black Americans what their white counterparts have. Wright and Du Bois agree: they are not the problem because they do not have the power.

FROM W.E.B. DU BOIS, *THE SOULS OF BLACK FOLK* (1903)

Chapter 1

Of Our Spiritual Strivings

Between me and the other world there is ever an unasked question: unasked by some through feelings of delicacy; by others through the difficulty of rightly framing it. All, nevertheless, flutter round it. They approach me in a half-hesitant sort of way, eye me curiously or compassionately, and then, instead of saying directly, How does it feel to be a problem? They say, I know an excellent colored man in my town; or, I fought at Mechanicsville; or, Do not these Southern outrages make your blood boil? At these I smile, or am interested, or reduce the boiling to a simmer, as the occasion may require. To the real question, How does it feel to be a problem? I answer seldom a word.

And yet, being a problem is a strange experience,—peculiar even for one who has never been anything else, save perhaps in babyhood and in Europe. It is in the early days of rollicking boyhood that the revelation first bursts upon one, all in a day, as it were. I remember well when the shadow swept across me. I was a little thing, away up in the hills of New England, where the dark Housatonic winds between Hoosac and Taghkanic to the sea. In a wee wooden schoolhouse, something put it into the boys' and girls' heads to buy gorgeous visiting-cards—ten cents a package—and exchange. The exchange was merry, till one girl, a tall newcomer, refused my card,—refused it peremptorily, with a glance. Then it dawned upon me with a certain suddenness that I was different from the others; or like, mayhap, in heart and life and longing, but shut out from their world by a vast veil. I had thereafter no desire to tear down that veil, to creep through; I held all beyond it in common contempt, and lived above it in a region of blue sky and great wandering shadows. That sky was bluest when I could beat my mates at examination-time, or beat them at a foot-race, or even beat their stringy heads. Alas, with the years all this fine contempt began to fade; for the worlds I longed for and all their dazzling opportunities, were theirs, not mine. But they should not keep these prizes, I said; some, all, I would wrest from them. Just how I would do it I could never decide: by reading law, by healing the sick, by telling the wonderful tales that swam in my head,—some way. With other black boys the strife was not so fiercely sunny: their youth shrunk into tasteless sycophancy, or into silent hatred of the pale world about them and mocking distrust of everything white; or wasted itself in a bitter cry, Why did God make me an outcast and a stranger in mine own house? The shades of the prison-house closed round about us all: walls strait and stubborn to the whitest, but relentlessly narrow, tall, and unscalable to sons of night who must plod darkly on in resignation, or beat unavailing palms against the stone, or steadily, half hopelessly, watch the streak of blue above.

After the Egyptian and Indian, the Greek and Roman, the Teuton and Mongolian, the Negro is a sort of seventh son, born with a veil, and gifted with second-sight in this American world,—a world which yields him no true self-consciousness, but only lets him see himself through the revelation of the other world. It is a peculiar sensation, this double-consciousness, this sense of always looking at one's soul by the tape of a world that looks on in amused contempt and pity. One ever feels his twoness,—an American, a Negro; two souls, two thoughts, two unreconciled strivings; two warring ideals in one dark body, whose dogged strength alone keeps it from being torn asunder.

The history of the American Negro is the history of this strife,—this longing to attain self-conscious manhood, to merge his double self into a better and truer self. In this merging he wishes neither of the older selves to be lost. He would not Africanize America, for America has too much to teach the world and Africa. He would not bleach his Negro soul in a flood of white Americanism, for he knows that Negro blood has a message for the world. He simply wishes to make it possible for a man to be both a Negro and an American, without having the doors of Opportunity closed roughly in his face.

This, then, is the end of his striving; to be a co-worker in the kingdom of culture, to escape both death and isolation, to husband and use his best powers and his latent genius. These powers of body and mind have in the past been strangely wasted, dispersed, or forgotten. The shadow of a mighty Negro past flits through the tale of Ethiopia the Shadowy and of Egypt the Sphinx. Throughout history, the powers of single black men flash here and there like falling stars, and die sometimes before the world has rightly gauged their brightness. Here in America, in the few days since Emancipation, the black man's turning hither and thither in hesitant and doubtful striving has often made his very strength to lose effectiveness, to seem like absence of power, like weakness. And yet it is not weakness,—it is the contradiction of double aims. The double-aimed struggle of the black artisan—on the one hand to escape white contempt for a nation of mere hewers of wood and drawers of water, and on the other hand to plough and nail and dig for a poverty-stricken horde—could only result in making him a poor craftsman, for he had but half a heart in either cause. By the poverty and ignorance of his people, the Negro minister or doctor was tempted toward quackery and demagogy; and by the criticism of the other world, toward ideals that made him ashamed of his lowly tasks. The would-be black *savant* was confronted by the paradox that the knowledge his people needed was a twice-told tale to his white neighbors, while the knowledge which would teach the white world was Greek to his own flesh and blood. The innate love of harmony and beauty that set the ruder souls of his people a-dancing and a-singing raised but confusion and doubt in the soul of the black artist; for the beauty revealed to him was the soul-beauty of a race which his larger audience despised, and he could not articulate the message of another people. This waste of double aims, this seeking to satisfy two unreconciled ideals, has wrought sad havoc with the courage and faith and deeds of ten thou-

sand people,—has sent them often wooing false gods and invoking false
means of salvation, and at times has even seemed about to make them
ashamed of themselves.

Away back in the days of bondage they thought to see in one divine
event the end of all doubt and disappointment; few men ever worshipped
freedom with half such unquestioning faith as did the American Negro
for two centuries. To him, so far as he thought and dreamed, slavery was
indeed the sum of all villainies, the cause of all sorrow, the root of all
prejudice; Emancipation was the key to a promised land of sweeter
beauty than ever stretched before the eyes of wearied Israelites. In song
and exhortation swelled one refrain—Liberty; in his tears and curses the
God he implored had Freedom in his right hand. At last it came,—suddenly, fearfully, like a dream. With one wild carnival of blood and passion
came the message in his own plaintive cadences:—

> Shout, O children!
> Shout, you're free!
> For God has bought your liberty!

Years have passed away since then,—ten, twenty, forty; forty years of
national life, forty years of renewal and development, and yet the swarthy
spectre sits in its accustomed seat at the Nation's feast. In vain do we cry
to this our vastest social problem:—

> Take any shape but that, and my firm nerves
> Shall never tremble!

The Nation has not yet found peace from its sins; the freedman has not
yet found in freedom his promised land. Whatever of good may have
come in these years of change, the shadow of a deep disappointment
rests upon the Negro people,—a disappointment all the more bitter because the unattained ideal was unbounded save by the simple ignorance
of a lowly people.

The first decade was merely a prolongation of the vain search for freedom, the boon that seemed ever barely to elude their grasp,—like a tan-
talizing will-o'-the-wisp, maddening and misleading the headless host.
The holocaust of war, the terrors of the Ku-Klux Klan, the lies of carpet-
baggers, the disorganization of industry, and the contradictory advice of
friends and foes, left the bewildered serf with no new watchword beyond
the old cry for freedom. As the time flew, however, he began to grasp a
new idea. The ideal of liberty demanded for its attainment powerful
means, and these the Fifteenth Amendment gave him. The ballot, which
before he had looked upon as a visible sign of freedom, he now regarded
as the chief means of gaining and perfecting the liberty with which war

had partially endowed him. And why not? Had not votes made war and emancipated millions? Had not votes enfranchised the freedmen? Was anything impossible to a power that had done all this? A million black men started with renewed zeal to vote themselves into the kingdom. So the decade flew away, the revolution of 1876 came, and left the half-free serf weary, wondering but still inspired. Slowly but steadily, in the following years, a new vision began gradually to replace the dream of political power,—a powerful movement, the rise of another ideal to guide the unguided, another pillar of fire by night after a clouded day. It was the ideal of "book-learning"; the curiosity, born of compulsory ignorance, to know and test the power of the cabalistic letters of the white man, the longing to know. Here at last seemed to have been discovered the mountain path to Canaan; longer than the highway of Emancipation and law, steep and rugged, but straight, leading to heights high enough to overlook life.

Up the new path the advance guard toiled, slowly, heavily, doggedly; only those who have watched and guided the faltering feet, the misty minds, the dull understandings, of the dark pupils of these schools know how faithfully, how piteously, this people strove to learn. It was weary work. The cold statistician wrote down the inches of progress here and there, noted also where here and there a foot had slipped or some one had fallen. To the tired climbers, the horizon was ever dark, the mists were often cold, the Canaan was always dim and far away. If, however, the vistas disclosed as yet no goal, no resting-place, little but flattery and criticism, the journey at least gave leisure for reflection and self-examination; it changed the child of Emancipation to the youth with dawning self-consciousness, self-realization, self-respect. In those sombre forests of his striving his own soul rose before him, and he saw himself,— darkly as through a veil; and yet he saw in himself some faint revelation of his power, of his mission. He began to have a dim feeling that, to attain his place in the world, he must be himself, and not another. For the first time he sought to analyze the burden he bore upon his back, that deadweight of social degradation partially masked behind a half-named Negro problem. He felt his poverty; without a cent, without a home, without land, tools, or savings, he had entered into competition with rich, landed, skilled neighbors. To be a poor man is hard, but to be a poor race in a land of dollars is the very bottom of hardships. He felt the weight of his ignorance,—not simply of letters, but of life, of business, of the humanities; the accumulated sloth and shirking and awkwardness of decades and centuries shackled his hands and feet. Nor was his burden all poverty and ignorance. The red stain of bastardy, which two centuries of systemic legal defilement of Negro women had stamped upon his race, meant not only the loss of ancient African chastity, but also the hereditary weight of a mass of corruption from white adulterers, threatening almost the obliteration of the Negro home.

A people thus handicapped ought not to be asked to race with the world, but rather allowed to give all its time and thought to its own social problems. But alas! while sociologists gleefully count his bastards and his prostitutes, the very soul of the toiling, sweating black man is darkened by the shadow of a vast despair. Men call the shadow prejudice, and learnedly explain it as the natural defence of culture against barbarism, learning against the "lower" races. To which the Negro cries Amen! and swears that to so much of this strange prejudice as is founded on just homage to civilization, culture, righteousness, and progress, he humbly bows and meekly does obeisance. But before that nameless prejudice that leaps beyond all this he stands helpless, dismayed, and well-nigh speechless; before that personal disrespect and mockery, the ridicule and systematic humiliation, the distortion of fact and wanton license of fancy, the cynical ignoring of the better and the boisterous welcoming of the worse, the all-pervading desire to inculcate disdain of everything black, from Toussaint to the devil,—before this there rises a sickening despair that would disarm and discourage any nation save that black host to whom "discouragement" is an unwritten word.

But the facing of so vast a prejudice could not but bring the inevitable self-questioning, self-disparagement, and lowering of ideals which ever accompany repression and breed in an atmosphere of contempt and hate. Whispering and portents came borne upon the four winds: Lo! we are diseased and dying, cried the dark hosts; we cannot write, our voting is vain; what need of education, since we must always cook and serve? And the Nation echoed and enforced this self-criticism, saying: Be content to be servants, and nothing more; what need of higher culture for half-men? Away with the black man's ballot, by force or fraud,—and behold the suicide of a race! Nevertheless, out of the evil came something of good,— the more careful adjustment of education to real life, the clearer perception of the Negroes' social responsibilities, and the sobering realization of the meaning of progress.

So dawned the time of *Sturm und Drang*: storm and stress to-day rocks our little boat on the mad waters of the world-sea; there is within and without the sound of conflict, the burning of body and rending of soul; inspiration strives with doubt, and faith with vain questionings. The bright ideals of the past,—physical freedom, political power, the training of brains and the training of hands,—all these in turn have waxed and waned, until even the last grows dim and overcast. Are they all wrong,— all false? No, not that, but each alone was over-simple and incomplete,— the dreams of credulous race-childhood, or the fond imaginings of the other world which does not know and does not want to know our power. To be really true, all these ideals must be melted and welded into one. The training of the schools we need to-day more than ever,—the training of deft hands, quick eyes and ears, and above all the broader, deeper, higher culture of gifted minds and pure hearts. The power of the ballot we need in sheer self-defence,—else what shall save us from a second slavery? Freedom, too, the long-sought, we still seek,—the freedom of life and limb, the freedom to work and think, the freedom to love and aspire. Work, culture, liberty,—all these we need, not singly but together, not successively but together, each growing and aiding each, and all striving toward that vaster ideal that swims before the Negro people, the ideal of human brotherhood, gained through the unifying ideal of Race; the ideal of fostering and developing the traits and talents of the Negro, not in opposition to or contempt for other races, but rather in large conformity to the greater ideals of the American Republic, in order that some day on American soil two world-races may give each to each those character-istics both so sadly lack. We the darker ones come even now not alto-gether empty-handed: there are to-day no truer exponents of the pure human spirit of the Declaration of Independence than the American Ne-groes; there is no true American music but the wild sweet melodies of the Negro slave; the American fairy tales and folk-lore are Indian and African; and, all in all, we black men seem the sole oasis of simple faith and reverence in a dusty desert of dollars and smartness. Will America be poorer if she replace her brutal dyspeptic blundering with light-hearted but determined Negro humility? or her coarse and cruel wit with loving jovial good-humor? or her vulgar music with the soul of the Sorrow Songs?

Merely a concrete test of the underlying principles of the great republic is the Negro Problem, and the spiritual striving of the freedmen's sons is the travail of souls whose burden is almost beyond the measure of their strength, but who bear it in the name of an historic race, in the name of this the land of their fathers' fathers, and in the name of human oppor-tunity.

And now what I have briefly sketched in large outline let me on coming pages tell again in many ways, with loving emphasis and deeper detail, that men may listen to the striving in the souls of black folk.

Chicago: A. C. McClurg and Co.

STUDY QUESTIONS

1. Which autobiography does Wright's most resemble, that of Franklin, Douglass, Washington, or Du Bois?
2. Which narrator—Franklin, Douglass, Washington, Du Bois, or Wright—do you trust as the most faithful to factual truth, and why?
3. Which of these autobiographers do you admire most, and why?
4. Describe and explain differences in writing styles of these excerpts in terms of syntax, language, references and allusions, level of difficulty, tone.
5. What is the governing myth in Franklin? Douglass? Washington? Du Bois? Wright?
6. Why are these authors still read today?
7. Are any of these autobiographies examples or models of how to live? Why or why not?
8. Who are the intended audiences for these autobiographies? Explain the differences in these audiences.
9. If you wrote your autobiography, how would it be similar to and different from the autobiographies excerpted here?

TOPICS FOR WRITTEN OR ORAL EXPLORATION

1. Select class members to represent Franklin, Douglass, Washington, Du Bois, and Wright. Ask them to debate the relative merits of their different values and writing styles, as revealed in the excerpts in this chapter.
2. Ask your female classmates for their reactions to these autobiographies. Account for the differences between their reactions and those of your male classmates.
3. Read the complete version of one of the books excerpted in this chapter. Write a paper in which you compare and contrast it to *Black Boy*.
4. Discuss how much (or little) Wright seems to owe to his predecessors.
5. Why is *Black Boy* one of the most noteworthy autobiographies ever written by an American? In what ways does it differ from other famous autobiographies by Americans?

SUGGESTED READINGS

Adams, Henry. *The Education of Henry Adams*. New York: Modern Library, 1997.

Angelou, Maya. *I Know Why the Caged Bird Sings*. New York: Random House, 1996.

Brown, Claude. *Manchild in the Promised Land*. New York: Macmillan, 1965.

Brown, William Wells. *Narrative of William W. Brown, a Fugitive Slave*. New York: Johnson Reprint, 1970.

Cleaver, Eldridge. *Soul on Ice*. New York: Dell, 1970.

Douglass, Frederick. *Life and Times of Frederick Douglass*. Hartford, Conn.: Park, 1984.

———. *My Bondage and My Freedom*. Urbana: University of Illinois Press, 1987.

Equiano, Olaudah. *The Interesting Narrative of the Life of Olaudah Equiano*. New York: St. Martin's Press, 1995.

Jacobs, Harriet A. *Incidents in the Life of a Slave Girl, Written by Herself*. Edited by Jean Fagan Yellin. Cambridge, Mass.: Harvard University Press, 1987.

Johnson, James Weldon. *Along This Way*. New York: Viking Press, 1933.

Thurber, James. *My Life and Hard Times*. New York: HarperCollins, 1991.

X, Malcolm. *The Autobiography of Malcolm X*. New York: Random House, 1992.

3

The American Dream of Success

Black Boy can be viewed profitably as an extended conversation with an idea that has often been laughed at, but that nonetheless will not go away: the notion that in America everyone has a chance to fulfill the American dream—to make it, to get ahead, to go as far as his or her talents will allow. No matter what one's disadvantages at birth, so the theory maintains, a determined and resourceful person can succeed in America. What is meant by "success" is an issue that has never been resolved, but that lack of resolution does not seem to have weakened belief in the concept. It has been a driving concept in American literature for over two hundred years, and *Black Boy* was written in its wake, regardless of how much Wright might challenge that claim.

The concept of the American dream has promoted some controversial values. Is material self-interest, for example, a particularly noble goal? How much money is enough? An obsession with financial gain might distract one from pursuing other worthwhile goals, such as knowing and understanding other people. How many corners should one cut to achieve one's dream of success? How much does the American dream exclude those who are indifferent to getting ahead in the material sense or those who are not adept at it? Wright does not seem to have worried much about the last question at all. Very, very few people have the determination, energy, and resourcefulness Wright had.

Black Boy has an ambiguous relationship with the American dream of success, challenging it while at the same time being a product of it. The overall movement of the book is toward success of some kind, even in the unexpurgated version, where Part One ends on a much less upbeat note than in the expurgated version. The author is criticizing an idea that may have a stronger grip on him than he realizes. Wright's autobiography is thus part of a tradition in American literature that includes F. Scott Fitzgerald's *The Great Gatsby*, the Horatio Alger series, George Randolph Chester's Get-Rich-Quick Wallingford series, and many other works.

A cornerstone to this popular complex of ideas is the Declaration of Independence, which its author, Thomas Jefferson, himself a slaveowner, intended to apply to a select group of other white males, apparently not realizing that its arguments could be appropriated by anyone. If Jefferson has innate worth and dignity, why not his fellow African Americans, too? Wright took Jefferson's ideas seriously, unlike most of the white people in *Black Boy*. One of Wright's greatest frustrations in the book is that he knows he has just as much human worth as any of the whites do, but he also knows that most of them cannot see a truth that has to be taken on faith, something that cannot be proved, especially to those who have something to lose: if simply being "white" does not make one superior, then what is the basis for white supremacy? Nevertheless, Wright knows all too well what happens when he takes Jefferson's claim about equality seriously in front of whites.

Also included in this chapter is another document that figures prominently in the development of the idea of the American dream of success, "What Is an American?," from J. Hector St. Jean de Crèvecoeur's *Letters from an American Farmer* (1782). In Crèvecoeur's portrait of a society in which the only constraint on achievement is one's own efforts, African Americans are absent. What Crèvecoeur really means by an American is a European immigrant or his descendant who lives in America.

A major element in the legal foundation for the American dream of success is the Constitution, and for black Americans that means in particular the Thirteenth, Fourteenth, and Fifteenth Amendments. The Thirteenth Amendment abolished slavery based on law, but in Mississippi, where much of *Black Boy* is set, African Americans were second-class citizens until the 1960s. From their point of view, the South won the Civil War. The situation was similar with the Fourteenth Amendment (guaranteeing due process and equal protection under the law) and the Fifteenth Amendment (guaranteeing the right to vote): the Mississippi Constitution of 1890 eviscerated both amendments, in many ways leaving black Mississippians pretty much where they were before the end of the Civil War in 1865.

And yet, as *Black Boy* makes clear, even with all these obstacles to achieving the American dream, Wright still felt its tug: he too dreamed of commercial success. A popular treatment of the idea from a white point of view is found in George Randolph Chester's *Get-Rich-Quick Wallingford*, which appeared in 1907, a year before Wright was born. Wright wanted to save enough money to leave the South, becoming part of the Great Migration. To do this, he engaged in petty crime such as reselling theater tickets. Chester's J. Rufus Wallingford, as an American business buccaneer, has far more ambitious plans, as the excerpt from *Get-Rich-Quick Wallingford* indicates.

THE DECLARATION OF INDEPENDENCE

One of the central documents of American democracy, the Declaration of Independence informs Wright's autobiography from beginning to end. It could well serve as a political statement for the black community, with the white community playing the role of England; one of its most strategic omissions is any reference to the slaves. Jefferson objects to taxation without consent, and yet after 1865 African Americans were not only taxed without their consent, but saw a disproportionate amount of those taxes spent in the white community. The American dream of success, as Wright makes painfully clear, applies to white males, a minority, not to everybody, although the reader will note Jefferson's use of the inclusive "we."

Also noteworthy is what results when Jefferson's statements that "all men are created equal" and that they have the unalienable rights of life, liberty, and the pursuit of happiness are put into conversation with *Black Boy*. Wright implicitly but persistently raises the question, Why are these powerful ideas monopolized by a small fraction of the American population? An issue neither Jefferson nor Wright addresses is whether equality and liberty, whatever they might mean, can be combined. That is to say, will there not be less equality if there is more liberty, and more equality if there is less liberty?

THE DECLARATION OF INDEPENDENCE (1776)

In Congress, July 4, 1776,
THE UNANIMOUS DECLARATION OF THE THIRTEEN UNITED STATES OF AMERICA
    When in the Course of human events, it becomes necessary for one people to dissolve the political bands which have connected them with another, and to assume among the powers of the earth, the separate and equal station to which the Laws of Nature and of Nature's God entitle them, a decent respect to the opinions of mankind requires that they should declare the causes which impel them to the separation.—We hold these truths to be self-evident, that all men are created equal, that they are endowed by their Creator with certain unalienable Rights, that among

these are Life, Liberty, and the pursuit of Happiness.—That to secure these rights, Governments are instituted among Men, deriving their just powers from the consent of the governed—That whenever any Form of Government becomes destructive of these ends, it is the Right of the People to alter or to abolish it, and to institute new Government, laying its foundation on such principles and organizing its powers in such form, as to them shall seem most likely to effect their Safety and Happiness. Prudence, indeed, will dictate that Governments long established should not be changed for light and transient causes; and accordingly all experience hath shewn, that mankind are more disposed to suffer, while evils are sufferable, than to right themselves by abolishing the forms to which they are accustomed. But when a long train of abuses and usurpations, pursuing invariably the same Object, evinces a design to reduce them under absolute Despotism, it is their right, it is their duty, to throw off such Government, and to provide new Guards for their future security.— Such has been the patient sufferance of these Colonies; and such is now the necessity which constrains them to alter their former Systems of Government. The history of the present King of Great Britain is a history of repeated injuries and usurpations, all having in direct object the establishment of an absolute Tyranny over these States. To prove this, let Facts be submitted to a candid world.—He has refused his Assent to Laws, the most wholesome and necessary for the public good.—He has forbidden his Governors to pass Laws of immediate and pressing importance, unless suspended in their operation till This Assent should be obtained; and when so suspended, he has utterly neglected to attend to them.—He has refused to pass other Laws for the accommodation of large districts of people, unless those people would relinquish the right of Representation in the Legislature, a right inestimable to them and formidable to tyrants only.—He has called together legislative bodies at places unusual, uncomfortable, and distant from the depository of their public Records, for the sole purpose of fatiguing them into compliance with his measures.— He has dissolved Representative Houses repeatedly, for opposing with manly firmness his invasions on the rights of the people.—He has refused for a long time, after such dissolutions, to cause others to be elected; whereby the Legislative powers, incapable of Annihilation, have returned to the People at large for their exercise; the State remaining in the mean time exposed to all the dangers of invasion from without, and convulsions within.—He has endeavoured to prevent the population of these States; for that purpose obstructing the Laws of Naturalization of Foreigners; refusing to pass others to encourage their migrations hither, and raising the conditions of new Appropriations of Lands.—He has obstructed the Administration of Justice, by refusing his Assent to Laws for establishing Judiciary powers.—He has made Judges dependent on his

Will alone, for the tenure of their offices, and the amount and payment of their salaries.—He has erected a multitude of New Offices, and sent hither swarms of Officers to harass our People, and eat out their substance.—He has kept among us, in times of peace, Standing Armies without the Consent of our legislatures.—He has affected to render the Military independent of and superior to the Civil power.—He has combined with others to subject us to a jurisdiction foreign to our constitution, and unacknowledged by our laws; giving his Assent to their Acts of pretended Legislation—For Quartering large bodies of armed troops among us:—For protecting them, by a mock Trial, from Punishment for any Murders which they should commit on the Inhabitants of these States:—For cutting off our Trade with all parts of the world:—For imposing Taxes on us without our Consent:—For depriving us in many cases, of the benefits of Trial by Jury:—For transporting us beyond Seas to be tried for pretended offences:—For abolishing the free System of English Laws in a neighbouring Province, establishing therein an Arbitrary government, and enlarging its Boundaries so as to render it at once an example and fit instrument for introducing the same absolute rule into these Colonies:—For taking away our Charters, abolishing our most valuable Laws, and altering fundamentally the Forms of our Governments:—For suspending our own Legislatures, and declaring themselves invested with power to legislate for us in all cases whatsoever.—He has abdicated Government here, by declaring us out of his Protection and waging War against us:—He has plundered our seas, ravaged our Coasts, burnt our towns, and destroyed the Lives of our people.—He is at this time transporting large armies of foreign mercenaries to complete the works of death, desolation and tyranny, already begun with circumstances of Cruelty & perfidy scarcely paralleled in the most barbarous ages, and totally unworthy the Head of a civilized nation.—He has constrained our fellow Citizens taken Captive on the high Seas to bear Arms against their Country, to become the executioners of their friends and Brethren, or to fall themselves by their Hands.—He has excited domestic insurrections amongst us, and has endeavored to bring on the inhabitants of our frontiers, the merciless Indian Savages, whose known rule of warfare, is an undistinguished destruction of all ages, sexes and conditions. In every stage of these Oppressions We have Petitioned for Redress in the most humble terms: Our repeated Petitions have been answered only by repeated injury. A Prince, whose character is thus marked by every act which may define a Tyrant, is unfit to be the ruler of a free people. Nor have We been wanting in attentions to our British brethren. We have warned them from time to time of attempts by their legislature to extend an unwarrantable jurisdiction over us. We have reminded them of the circumstances of our emigration and settlement here. We have appealed to their native justice and magnanimity, and we have conjured them by the ties of our common kindred to disavow these usurpations, which would inevitably interrupt our connections and correspondence. They too have been deaf to the voice of justice and of consanguinity. We must, therefore, acquiesce in the necessity, which denounces our Separation, and hold them, as we hold the rest of mankind, Enemies in War, in Peace Friends.

WE, THEREFORE, the Representatives of the UNITED STATES OF AMERICA, in General Congress, Assembled, appealing to the Supreme Judge of the world for the rectitude of our intentions, do, in the Name, and by Authority of the good People of these Colonies, solemnly publish and declare, That these United Colonies are, and of Right ought to be FREE AND INDEPENDENT STATES; that they are Absolved from all Allegiance to the British Crown, and that all political connection between them and the State of Great Britain, is and ought to be totally dissolved; and that as Free and Independent States, they have full Power to levy War, conclude Peace, contract Alliances, establish Commerce, and to do all other Acts and Things which Independent States may of right do. And for the support of this Declaration, with a firm reliance on the Protection of Divine Providence, we mutually pledge to each other our Lives, our Fortunes and our sacred Honor.

A FORBIDDEN TOPIC

Wright notes that among the topics white men did not discuss with blacks were the Thirteenth, Fourteenth, and Fifteenth Amendments to the Constitution. Adopted in 1865, 1868, and 1870, respectively, these amendments were designed to abolish slavery, guarantee due process and equal protection under the law, and make blacks eligible to vote. In fact, especially in Mississippi, these changes in the Constitution, which should have helped blacks gain access to the American dream of success, did nothing of the kind. After Reconstruction ended, most blacks were virtual slaves, did not enjoy due process and equal protection under the law, and could not vote. In many ways, they were no closer to realizing the American dream after the Civil War than before, as Wright realized so bitterly in *Black Boy*.

All three amendments were circumvented by establishing a system in which slavery was all but legal, as *Black Boy* makes clear. After the Civil War, Black Codes were enacted by southern state legislatures to control black people and deny them civil rights. These codes included vagrancy provisions that forced blacks to continue to perform manual labor for white employers. The codes recognized the legality of marriages between African Americans but prohibited interracial marriages and forbade blacks to serve on juries; some even denied blacks the right to rent land.

The 1890 Mississippi Constitution denied the state's black "citizens" civil rights until the 1960s, when national civil rights legislation was passed that did enable blacks to vote and hold public office, something that seems almost impossible from the perspective of *Black Boy*. Moreover, through the lynchings, floggings, beatings, and shootings of black people, the Ku Klux Klan, the Knights of the White Camellia, the White Brotherhood, and numerous other white terrorist organizations saw to it that the constitutional amendments reprinted in this chapter remained futile gestures. The famous 1896 Supreme Court decision *Plessy v. Ferguson*, which upheld the legality of segregated "separate but equal" public facilities, resulted, among other things, in the inferior formal schooling Wright received. By the time Wright was born in 1908, few black Southerners enjoyed anything like the political, social, economic, or educational opportunities available to whites.

THE THIRTEENTH, FOURTEENTH, AND FIFTEENTH AMENDMENTS TO THE CONSTITUTION (1865, 1868, and 1870)

[Amendment xiii]

Section 1.
[Abolition of Slavery]

Neither slavery nor involuntary servitude, except as a punishment for crime whereof the party shall have been duly convicted, shall exist within the United States, or any place subject to their jurisdiction.

Section 2.
[Power to Enforce This Article]

Congress shall have power to enforce this article by appropriate legislation.

[Amendment xiv]

Section 1.
[Citizenship Rights Not to Be Abridged by States]

All persons born or naturalized in the United States, and subject to the jurisdiction thereof, are citizens of the United States and of the State wherein they reside. No State shall make or enforce any law which shall abridge the privileges or immunities of citizens of the United States; nor shall any State deprive any person of life, liberty, or property, without due process of law; nor deny to any person within its jurisdiction the equal protection of the laws.

Section 2.
[Appointment of Representatives in Congress]

Representatives shall be apportioned among the several States according to their respective numbers, counting the whole number of persons in each State, excluding Indians not taxed. But when the right to vote at any election for the choice of electors for President and Vice-President of the United States, Representatives in Congress, the Executive and Judicial officers of a State, or the members of the Legislature thereof, is denied to any of the male inhabitants of such State, being twenty-one years of age, and citizens of the United States, or in any way abridged, except for participation in rebellion, or other crime, the basis of representation therein shall be reduced in the proportion which the number of such male citizens shall bear to the whole number of male citizens twenty-one years of age in such State.

Section 3.
[*Persons Disqualified from Holding Office*]

No person shall be a Senator or Representative in Congress, or elector of President and Vice-President, or hold any office, civil or military, under the United States, or under any State, who, having previously taken an oath, as a member of Congress, or as an officer of the United States, or as a member of any State legislature, or as an executive or judicial officer of any State, to support the Constitution of the United States, shall have engaged in insurrection or rebellion against the same, or given aid or comfort to the enemies thereof. But Congress may by a vote of two-thirds of each House, remove such disability.

Section 4.
[*What Public Debts Are Valid*]

The validity of the public debt of the United States, authorized by law, including debts incurred for payment of pensions and bounties for services in suppressing insurrection or rebellion, shall not be questioned. But neither the United States nor any State shall assume or pay any debt or obligation incurred in aid of insurrection or rebellion against the United States, or any claim for the loss or emancipation of any slave; but all such debts, obligations and claims shall be held illegal and void.

Section 5.
[*Power to Enforce This Article*]

The Congress shall have power to enforce, by appropriate legislation, the provisions of this article.

[*Amendment xv*]

Section 1.
[*Negro Suffrage*]

The right of citizens of the United States to vote shall not be denied or abridged by the United States or by any State on account of race, color, or previous condition of servitude.

Section 2.
[*Power to Enforce This Article*]

The Congress shall have power to enforce this article by appropriate legislation.

WHAT IS AN AMERICAN?

In the following document, J. Hector St. Jean de Crèvecoeur sees evidence everywhere for the truth of Jefferson's vision of what an independent American would be like: he (Crèvecoeur's perspective is gender- as well as race-based) would be self-reliant, succeeding through his own efforts. Crèvecoeur universalizes the experiences of some European Americans, not caring to point out that most people in America in 1782, when *Letters from an American Farmer* appeared, were not European American males. Where Crèvecoeur flatters his reader's desire to believe in America as a kind of social utopia, Wright indignantly corrects him.

As an extended conversation with Crèvecoeur's letter, *Black Boy* is confronted by the very powerful assumption on the French writer's part, an assumption still influential now, that an American is a Christian, white, male. That is the unquestioned model that Wright is up against in *Black Boy*. A hidden model obviously cannot be challenged, but the point that Wright needs to make is that no model for what an American is is possible or even needed, because an American could be anyone who lives in America. Definitions, by their very nature, exclude as they include, and Crèvecoeur's unstated stereotype of what an American is excludes most people in America.

Crèvecoeur is fascinated, as have been so many other writers, by the first reactions of Europeans to their "discovery" of America. It never occurs to him, though, to imagine the reactions of Wright's West African ancestors as they arrived in America, on ships with names like *Mercy* and *Charity*. Nor does Crèvecoeur consider the reactions of Native Americans to the European "discovery" of America. He is completely blind to a society of Americans that included people who look like Richard Wright or his African and Native American forebears. Whereas Crèvecoeur sees unlimited opportunity for anyone willing to work hard, *Black Boy* depicts a society in which no matter how hard an African American works, he or she will not be rewarded as a white fellow American would be. What is so painfully ironic about Crèvecoeur's view is that although he can see the injustices in the way Europe treated its nonaristocrats, he cannot see that in America, women, Native Americans, and African Americans are treated unjustly. For Crèvecoeur to see the irony here, he would have to rethink his ideas of what an American is. One of Wright's goals in *Black Boy* is to expand that definition to include black *men*, if no one else. Even a half-century after the publication of *Black Boy*, every American president fits Crèvecoeur's description of what an American is.

FROM J. HECTOR ST. JEAN DE CRÈVECOEUR, "WHAT IS AN AMERICAN?" (1782)

I wish I could be acquainted with the feelings and thoughts which must agitate the heart and present themselves to the mind of an enlightened Englishman, when he first lands on this continent. He must greatly rejoice that he lived at a time to see this fair country discovered and settled; he must necessarily feel a share of national pride, when he views the chain of settlements which embellishes these extended shores. When he says to himself, this is the work of my countrymen, who, when convulsed by factions, afflicted by a variety of miseries and wants, restless and impatient, took refuge here. They brought along with them their national genius, to which they principally owe what liberty they enjoy, and what substance they possess. Here he sees the industry of his native country displayed in a new manner, and traces in their works the embryos of all the arts, sciences, and ingenuity which flourish in Europe. Here he beholds fair cities, substantial villages, extensive fields, an immense country filled with decent houses, good roads, orchards, meadows, and bridges, where an hundred years ago all was wild, woody, and uncultivated! What a train of pleasing ideas this fair spectacle must suggest; it is a prospect which must inspire a good citizen with the most heartfelt pleasure. The difficulty consists in the manner of viewing so extensive a scene. He is arrived on a new continent; a modern society offers itself to his contemplation, different from what he had hitherto seen. It is not composed, as in Europe, of great lords who possess everything, and of a herd of people who have nothing. Here are no aristocratical families, no courts, no kings, no bishops, no ecclesiastical dominion, no invisible power giving to a few a very visible one; no great manufacturers employing thousands, no great refinements of luxury. The rich and the poor are not so far removed from each other as they are in Europe. Some few towns excepted, we are all tillers of the earth, from Nova Scotia to West Florida. We are a people of cultivators, scattered over an immense territory, communicating with each other by means of good roads and navigable rivers, united by the silken bands of mild government, all respecting the laws, without dreading their power, because they are equitable. We are all animated with the spirit of an industry which is unfettered and unrestrained, because each person works for himself. If he travels through our rural districts he views not the hostile castle, and the haughty mansion, contrasted with the clay-built hut and miserable cabin, where cattle and men help to keep each other warm, and dwell in meanness, smoke, and indigence. A pleasing uniformity of decent competence appears throughout our habitations. The meanest of our log-houses is a dry and comfortable habituation. Lawyer or merchant are the fairest titles our towns afford; that of a farmer is the only appellation of the rural inhabitants of our country. It must take some time ere he can reconcile himself to our dictionary, which is but short in words of dignity, and names of honour. There, on a Sunday, he sees a congregation of respectable farmers and their wives, all clad in neat homespun, well mounted, or riding in their own humble wagons. There is not among them an esquire, saving the unlettered magistrate. There he sees a parson as simple as his flock, a farmer who does not riot on the labour of others. We have no princes, for whom we toil, starve, and bleed: we are the most perfect society now existing in the world. Here man is free as he ought to be; nor is this pleasing equality so tran-sitory as many others are. Many ages will not see the shores of our great lakes replenished with inland nations, nor the unknown bounds of North America entirely peopled. Who can tell how far it extends? Who can tell the millions of men whom it will feed and contain? for no European foot has as yet traveled half the extent of this mighty continent!

The next wish of this traveler will be to know whence came all these people? they are a mixture of English, Scotch, Irish, French, Dutch, Ger-mans, and Swedes. From this promiscuous breed, that race now called Americans have arisen. The eastern provinces must indeed be excepted, as being the unmixed descendants of Englishmen. I have heard many wish that they had been more intermixed also: for my part, I am no wisher, and think it much better as it has happened. They exhibit a most conspicuous figure in this great and variegated picture; they too enter for a great share in the pleasing perspective displayed in these thirteen provinces. I know it is fashionable to reflect on them, but I respect them for what they have done; for the accuracy and wisdom with which they have settled their territory; for the decency of their manners; for their early love of letters; their ancient college, the first in this hemisphere; for their industry; which to me who am but a farmer, is the criterion of everything. There never was a people, situated as they are, who with so ungrateful a soil have done more in so short a time. Do you think that the monarchical ingredients which are more prevalent in other govern-ments, have purged them from all foul stains? Their histories assert the contrary.

In this great American asylum, the poor of Europe have by some means met together, and in consequence of various causes; to what purpose should they ask one another what countrymen they are? Alas, two thirds of them had no country. Can a wretch who wanders about, who works and starves, whose life is a continual scene of sore affliction or pinching penury; can that man call England or any other kingdom his country? A country that had no bread for him, whose fields procured him no harvest, who met with nothing but the frowns of the rich, the severity of the laws, with jails and punishments; who owned not a single foot of the extensive surface of this planet? No! urged by a variety of motives, here they came. Every thing has tended to regenerate them; new laws, a new mode of living, a new social system; here they are become men: in Europe they were as so many useless plants, wanting vegetative mould, and refreshing showers; they withered, and were mowed down by want, hunger, and war; but now by the power of transplantation, like all other plants they have taken root and flourished! Formerly they were not numbered in any civil lists of their country, except in those of the poor; here they rank as citizens. By what invisible power has this surprising metamorphosis been performed? By that of the laws and that of their industry. The laws, the indulgent laws, protect them as they arrive, stamping on them the symbol of adoption; they receive ample rewards for their labours; these accumulated rewards procure them lands; those lands confer on them the title of freemen, and to that title every benefit is affixed which men can possibly require. This is the great operation daily performed by our laws. From whence proceed these laws? From our government. Whence the government? It is derived from the original genius and strong desire of the people ratified and confirmed by the crown. This is the great chain which links us all, this is the picture which every province exhibits, Nova Scotia excepted. There the crown has done all; either there were no people who had genius, or it was not much attended to: the consequence is, that the province is very thinly inhabited indeed; the power of the crown in conjunction with the musketos has prevented men from settling there. Yet some parts of it flourished once, and it contained a mild harmless set of people. But for the fault of a few leaders, the whole were banished. The greatest political error the crown ever committed in America, was to cut off men from a country which wanted nothing but men!

What attachment can a poor European emigrant have for a country where he had nothing? The knowledge of the language, the love of a few kindred as poor as himself, were the only cords that tied him; his country is now that which gives him land, bread, protection, and consequence: *Ubi panis ibi patria* [one's country is where one's bread is], is the motto of all emigrants. What then is the American, this new man? He is either an European, or the descendant of an European, hence that strange mixture of blood, which you will find in no other country. I could point out to you a family whose grandfather was an Englishman, whose wife was Dutch, whose son married a French woman, and whose present four sons have now four wives of different nations. *He* is an American, who, leaving behind him all his ancient prejudices and manners, receives new ones from the new mode of life he has embraced, the new government he obeys, and the new rank he holds. He becomes an American by being received in the broad lap of our great *Alma Mater*. Here individuals of all nations are melted into a new race of men, whose labours and posterity will one day cause great changes in the world. Americans are the western pilgrims, who are carrying along with them that great mass of arts, sciences, vigour, and industry which began long since in the east; they will finish the great circle. The Americans were once scattered all over Europe; here they are incorporated into one of the finest systems of population which has ever appeared, and which will hereafter become distinct by the power of the different climates they inhabit. *The* American ought therefore to love this country much better than that wherein either he or his forefathers were born. Here the rewards of his industry follow with equal steps the progress of his labour; his labour is founded on the basis of nature, *self-interest*; can it want a stronger allurement? Wives and children, who before in vain demanded of him a morsel of bread, now, fat, and frolicsome, gladly help their father to clear those fields whence exuberant crops are to arise to feed and to clothe them all; without any part being claimed, either by a despotic prince, a rich abbot, or a mighty lord. Here religion demands but little of him; a small voluntary salary to the minister, and gratitude to God; can he refuse these? The American is a new man, who acts upon new principles; he must therefore entertain new ideas, and form new opinions. From involuntary idleness, servile dependence, penury, and useless labour, he has passed to toils of a very different nature, rewarded by ample subsistence.—This is an American.

• • •

But how is this accomplished in that crowd of low, indigent people, who flock here every year from all parts of Europe? I will tell you; they no sooner arrive than they immediately feel the good effects of that plenty of provisions we possess: they fare on our best food, and they are kindly entertained; their talents, character, and peculiar industry are immediately inquired into; they find countrymen everywhere disseminated, let them come from whatever part of Europe. Let me select one as an epitome of the rest; he is hired, he goes to work, and works moderately; instead of being employed by a haughty person, he finds himself with his equal, placed at the substantial table of the farmer, or else at an inferior one as good; his wages are high, his bed is not like that bed of sorrow on which he used to lie: if he behaves with propriety, and is faithful, he is caressed, and becomes as it were a member of the family. He begins to feel the effects of a sort of resurrection; hitherto he had not lived, but simply vegetated; he now feels himself a man, because he is treated as such; the laws of his own country had overlooked him in his insignificancy; the laws of this cover him with their mantle. Judge what an alteration there must arise in the mind and thoughts of this man; he begins to forget his former servitude and dependence, his heart involuntarily swells and glows; this first swell inspires him with those new thoughts which constitute an American. What love can he entertain for a country where his existence was a burthen to him; if he is a generous good man, the love of this new adoptive parent will sink deep into his heart. He looks around, and sees many a prosperous person, who but a few years before was as poor as himself. This encourages him much, he begins to form some little scheme, the first, alas, he ever formed in his life. If he is wise he thus spends two or three years, in which time he acquires knowledge, the use of tools, the modes of working the lands, felling trees, etc. This prepares the foundation of a good name, the most useful acquisition he can make. He is encouraged, he has gained friends; he is advised and directed, he feels bold, he purchases some land; he gives all the money he has brought over, as well as what he has earned, and trusts to the God of harvests for the discharge of the rest. His good name procures him credit. He is now possessed of the deed, conveying to him and his posterity the fee simple and absolute property of two hundred acres of land, situated on such a river. What an epoch in this man's life! He is become a freeholder, from perhaps a German boor—he is now an American, a Pennsylvanian, and English subject. He is naturalized, his name is enrolled with those of the other citizens of the province. Instead of being a vagrant, he has a place of residence; he is called the inhabitant of such a country, or of such a district, and for the first time in his life counts for something; for hitherto he has been a cypher. I only repeat what I have heard many say, and no wonder their hearts should glow, and be agitated with a multitude of feelings, not easy to describe. From nothing to start into being; from a servant to the rank of a master; from being the slave of some despotic prince, to become a free man, invested with lands, to which every municipal blessing is annexed! What a change indeed! It is in consequence of that change that he becomes an American. This great metamorphosis has a double effect, it extinguishes all his European prejudices, he forgets that mechanism of subordination, that servility of disposition which poverty had taught him; and sometimes he is apt to forget too much, often passing from one extreme to the other. If he is a good man, he forms schemes of future prosperity, he proposes to educate his children better than he has been educated himself; he thinks of future modes of conduct, feels an ardour to labour he never felt before. Pride steps in and leads him to everything that the laws do not forbid: he respects them; with a heart-felt gratitude he looks toward the east, toward that insular government from whose wisdom all his new felicity is derived, and under whose wings and protection he now lives. These reflections constitute him the good man and the good subject. Ye poor Europeans, ye, who sweat, and work for the great—ye, who are obliged to give so many sheaves to the church, so many to your lords, so many to your government, and have hardly any left for yourselves— ye, who are held in less estimation than favourite hunters or useless lap- dogs—ye, who only breathe the air of nature, because it cannot be with- held from you; it is here that you can conceive the possibility of those feelings I have been describing; it is here the laws of naturalization invite everyone to partake of our great labours and felicity, to till unrented, untaxed lands! Many, corrupted beyond the power of amendment, have brought with them all their vices, and disregarding the advantages held to [them], have gone on in their former career of iniquity, until they have been overtaken and punished by our laws. It is not every emigrant who succeeds; no, it is only the sober, the honest, and industrious: happy those to whom this transition has served as a powerful spur to labour, to prosperity, and to the good establishment of children, born in the days of their poverty; and who had no other portion to expect but the rags of their parents, had it not been for their happy emigration. Others again, have been led astray by this enchanting scene; their new pride, instead of leading them to the fields, has kept them in idleness; the idea of possessing lands is all that satisfies them—though surrounded with fertility, they have mouldered away their time in inactivity, misinformed husbandry, and ineffectual endeavours. How much wiser, in general, the honest Germans than almost all other Europeans; they hire themselves to some of their wealthy landsmen, and in that apprenticeship learn everything that is necessary. They attentively consider the prosperous in- dustry of others, which imprints in their minds a strong desire of pos- sessing the same advantages. This forcible idea never quits them, they launch forth, and by dint of sobriety, rigid parsimony, and the most per- severing industry, they commonly succeed. Their astonishment at their first arrival from Germany is very great—it is to them a dream; the con- trast must be powerful indeed; they observe their countrymen flourishing in every place; they travel through whole counties where not a word of English is spoken; and in the names and the language of the people, they retrace Germany. They have been an useful acquisition to this continent, and to Pennsylvania in particular; to them it owes some share of its prosperity: to their mechanical knowledge and patience it owes the finest mills in all America, the best teams of horses, and many other advantages. The recollection of their former poverty and slavery never quits them as long as they live.

Letters from an American Farmer, Letter III (New York: E. P. Dutton, 1912).

MAKING IT IN AMERICA

The American dream of success has been such a resonant idea that it has been interpreted and realized in many different ways, from Benjamin Franklin's strategy to Jay Gatsby's in Fitzgerald's novel *The Great Gatsby* (Donald Trump could be taken as a contemporary exemplar). The year before Wright was born, George Randolph Chester published an interpretation of the American dream of success in *Get-Rich-Quick Wallingford*, part of a series that Wright mentions in *Black Boy* as having affected him. J. Rufus Wallingford believed in making money as quickly as possible, which meant illegally. Given the extremely frustrating situation Wright depicts in his autobiography, it is easy to understand his attraction to a get-rich-quick scheme, such as Wallingford's nonexistent Universal Covered Carpet Tack Company. Wright's money-making schemes are more modest—selling the same movie tickets twice and trying to profit from selling bootleg whiskey. And unlike Wallingford, Wright wants money in order to leave the South, not out of greed.

Wright does share with Wallingford faith in one aspect of making it in America: the value of using personal freedom for the purpose of self-realization. Wallingford is interested in Wallingford, just as Wright is interested in Wright; the other members of their communities are on their own. Although Wright was a member of the Communist Party for a while, he believes more in self-reliance than in group reliance. Like Wallingford, he wants to make it through his own efforts, on the basis of his own accomplishments. This is not to say that he is unconcerned about the black community, but that his primary focus is on his own struggle to realize his potential as a writer. In America, you make it on your own efforts. Neither Wright nor Wallingford thinks about the human costs involved in rugged individualism, because they are both so determined to reach material—and in Wright's case literary—goals in America.

FROM GEORGE RANDOLPH CHESTER, *GET-RICH-QUICK WALLINGFORD* (1907)

Chapter 1

In which J. Rufus Wallingford Conceives a Brilliant Invention

The mud was black and oily where it spread thinly at the edges of the asphalt, and wherever it touched it left a stain; it was upon the leather of every pedestrian, even the most fastidious, and it bordered with almost laughable conspicuousness the higher marking of yellow clay upon the heavy shoes of David Jasper, where he stood at the curb in front of the big hotel with his young friend, Edward Lamb. Absorbed in "lodge" talk, neither of the oddly assorted cronies cared much for a drizzle overhead or mire underfoot; but a splash of black mud in the face must necessarily command some attention. This surprise came suddenly to both from the circumstance of a cab having dashed up just beside them. Their resentment, bubbling hot for a moment, was quickly chilled, however, as the cab door opened and out of it stepped one of those impressive beings for whom the best things of this world have been especially made and provided. He was a large gentleman, a suave gentleman, a gentleman whose clothes not merely fit him but distinguished him, a gentleman of rare good living, even though one of the sort whose faces turn red when they eat; and the dignity of his worldly prosperousness surrounded him like a blessed aura. Without a glance at the two plain citizens who stood mopping the mud from their faces, he strode majestically into the hotel, leaving Mr. David Jasper and Mr. Edward Lamb out in the rain.

The clerk kowtowed to the signature, though he had never seen nor heard of it before—"J. Rufus Wallingford, Boston." His eyes, however, had noted a few things: traveling suit, scarf pin, watch guard, ring, hatbox, suit case, bag, all expensive and of the finest grade.

"Sitting room and bedroom; outside!" directed Mr. Wallingford. "And the bathroom must have a large tub."

The clerk ventured a comprehending smile as he noted the bulk before him.

"Certainly, Mr. Wallingford. Boy, key for 44-A. Anything else, Mr. Wallingford?"

"Send up a waiter and a valet."

Once more the clerk permitted himself a slight smile, but this time it was as his large guest turned away. He had not the slightest doubt that Mr. Wallingford's bill would be princely, he was positive that it would be paid; but a vague wonder had crossed his mind as to who would regrettingly pay it. His penetration was excellent, for at this very moment the new arrival's entire capitalized worth was represented by the less than one hundred dollars he carried in his pocket, nor had Mr. Wallingford the slightest idea of where he was to get more. This latter circumstance did not distress him, however; he knew that there was still plenty of money in the world and that none of it was soldered on, and a reflection of this comfortable philosophy was in his whole bearing. As he strode in pomp across the lobby, a score of bellboys, with a carefully trained scent for tips, envied the cheerfully grinning servitor who followed him to the elevator with his luggage.

Just as the bellboy was inserting the key in the lock of 44-A, a tall, slightly built man in a glove-fitting black frock suit, a quite ministerial-looking man, indeed, had it not been for the startling effect of his extravagantly curled black mustache and his piercing black eyes, came down the hallway, so abstracted that he had almost passed Mr. Wallingford. The latter, however, had eyes for everything.

"What's the hurry, Blackie?" he inquired affably.

The other wheeled instantly, with the snappy alertness of a man who has grown of habit to hold himself in readiness against sudden surprises from any quarter.

"Hello, J. Rufus!" he exclaimed, and shook hands. "Boston squeezed dry?"

Mr. Wallingford chuckled with a cumbrous heaving of his shoulders.

"Just threw the rind away," he confessed. "Come in."

Mr. Daw, known as "Blackie" to a small but select circle of gentlemen who make it their business to rescue and put carefully hoarded money back into rapid circulation, dropped moodily into a chair and sat considering his well-manicured finger-nails in glum silence, while his masterful host disposed of the bellboy and the valet.

"Had your dinner?" inquired Mr. Wallingford as he donned the last few garments of a fresh suit.

"Not yet," growled the other. "I've got such a grouch against myself I won't even feed right, for fear I'd enjoy it. On the cheaps for the last day, too."

Mr. Wallingford laughed and shook his head.

"I'm clean myself," he hastened to inform his friend. "If I have a hundred I'm a millionaire, but I'm coming and you're going, and we don't look at that settle-up ceremony the same way. What's the matter?"

"I'm the goat!" responded Blackie moodily.

"The original goat! Came clear out here to trim a sucker that looked good by mail, and have swallowed so much of that citric fruit that if I scrape myself my skin spurts lemon juice. Say, do I look like a come-on?"

"If you only had the shaving-brush goatee, Blackie, I'd try to make you bet on the location of the little pea," gravely responded his friend.

"That's right; rub it in!" exclaimed the disgruntled one. "Massage me with it! Jimmy, if I could take off my legs, I'd kick myself with them from here to Boston and never lose a stroke. And me wise!"

"But where's the fire?" asked J. Rufus, bringing the end of his collar into place with a dexterous jerk.

"This lamb I came out to shear—rot him and burn him and scatter his ashes! Before I went dippy over two letter-heads and a nice round signature, I ordered an extra safety-deposit vault back home and came on to take his bank roll and house and lot, and make him a present of his clothes if he behaved. But not so! Not—so! Jimmy, this whole town blew right over from out of the middle of Missouri in the last cyclone. You've got to show everybody, and then turn it over and let 'em see the other side, and I haven't met the man yet that you could separate from a dollar without chloroform and an ax. Let me tell you what to do with that hundred, J. Rufe. Just get on the train and give it to the conductor, and tell him to take you as far ay-way from here as the money will reach!"

Mr. Wallingford settled his cravat tastefully and smiled at himself in the glass.

"I like the place," he observed. "They have tall buildings here, and I smell soft money. This town will listen to a legitimate business proposition. What?"

"Like the milk-stopper industry?" inquired Mr. Daw, grinning appreciatively. "How is your Boston corporation coming on, anyhow?"

"It has even quit holding the bag," responded the other, "because there isn't anything left of the bag. The last I saw of them, the thin and feeble stockholders were chasing themselves around in circles, so I faded away."

"You're a wonder," complimented the black haired man with genuine admiration. "You never take a chance, yet get away with everything in sight, and you never leave 'em an opening to put the funny clothes on you."

"I deal in nothing but straight commercial propositions that are strictly within the pale of the law," said J. Rufus without a wink; "and even at that they can't say I took anything away from Boston."

"Don't blame Boston. You never cleaned up a cent less than five thousand a month while you were there, and if you spent it, that was your lookout."

"I had to live."

"So do the suckers," sagely observed Mr. Daw, "but they manage it on four cents' worth of prunes a day, and save up their money for good people. How is Mrs. Wallingford?"

"All others are base imitations," boasted the large man, pausing to critically consider the flavor of his champagne. "Just now, Fanny's in New York, eating up her diamonds. She was swallowing the last of the brooch when I left her, and this morning she was to begin on the necklace. That ought to last her quite some days, and by that time J. Rufus expects to be on earth again."

A waiter came to the door with a menu card, and Mr. Wallingford ordered, to be ready to serve in three quarters of an hour, at a choice table near the music, a dinner for two that would gladden the heart of any tip-hunter.

"How soon are you going back to Boston, Blackie?"

"Tonight!" snapped the other. "I was going to take a train that makes it in nineteen hours, but I found there is one that makes it in eighteen and a half, so I'm going to take that; and when I get back where the police are satisfied with half, I'm not going after the emerald paper any more. I'm going to make them bring it to me. It's always the best way. I never went after money yet that they didn't ask me why I wanted it."

The large man laughed with his eyes closed.

"Honestly, Blackie, you ought to go into legitimate business enterprises. That's the only game. You can get anybody to buy stock when you make them print it themselves, if you'll only bait up with some little staple article that people use and throw away every day, like ice cream pails, or corks, or cigar bands, or—or—or carpet tacks." Having sought about the room for this last illustration, Mr. Wallingford became suddenly inspired, and, arising, went over to the edge of the carpet, where he gazed down meditatively for a moment. "Now, look at this, for instance!" he said with final enthusiasm. "See this swell red carpet fastened down with rusty tacks? There's the chance. Suppose those tacks were covered with red cloth to match the carpet. Blackie, that's my next invention."

"Maybe there are covered carpet tacks," observed his friend, with but languid interest.

"What do I care?" rejoined Mr. Wallingford. "A man can always get a patent, and that's all I need, even if it's one you can throw a cat through. The company can fight the patent after I'm out of it. You wouldn't expect me to fasten myself down to the grease-covered details of an actual manufacturing business, would you?"

"Not any!" rejoined the dark one emphatically. "You're all right, J. Rufus. I'd go into your business myself if I wasn't honest. But, on the level, what do you expect to do here?"

"Organize the Universal Covered Carpet Tack Company. I'll begin tomorrow morning. Give me the list you couldn't use."

"Don't get in bad from the start," warned Mr. Daw. "Tackle fresh ones. The particular piece of Roquefort, though, that fooled me into a Pullman compartment and kept me grinning like a drunken hyena all the way here, was a pinhead by the name of Edward Lamb. When Eddy fell for an inquiry about Billion Strike gold stock, he wrote on the firm's stationery, all printed in seventeen colors and embossed so it made holes in the envelopes when the cancellation stamp came down. From the tone of Eddy's letter I thought he was about ready to mortgage father's business to buy Billion Strike, and I came on to help him do it. Honest, J. Rufus, wouldn't it strike you that Lamb was a good name? Couldn't you hear it bleat?"

Mr. Wallingford shook silently, the more so that there was no answering gleam of mirth in Mr. Daw's savage visage.

"Say, do you know what I found when I got here?" went on Blackie still more ferociously. "I found he was a piker bookkeeper, but with five thousand dollars that he'd wrenched out of his own pay envelope, a pinch at a clip; and every time he takes a dollar out of his pocket his fingers creak. His whole push is like him, too, but I never got any further than Eddy. He's not merely Johnny Wise—he's the whole Wise family, and it's only due to my Christian bringing up that I didn't swat him with a brick during our last little chatter when I saw it all fade away. Do you know what he wanted me to do? He wanted me to prove to him that there actually was a Billion Strike mine, and that gold had been found in it!"

Mr. Wallingford had ceased to laugh. He was soberly contemplating.

"Your Lamb is my mutton," he finally concluded, pressing his finger tips together. "He'll listen to a legitimate business proposition."

"Don't make me fuss with you, J. Rufus," admonished Mr. Daw. "Remember, I'm going away to-night," and he arose.

Mr. Wallingford arose with him. "By the way, of course I'll want to refer to you; how many addresses have you besides the Billion Strike? A mention of that would probably get me arrested."

"Four: the Mexican and Rio Grande Rubber Company, Tremont Building; the St. John's Blood Orange Plantation Company, 643 Third Street; the Los Pocos Lead Development Company, 868 Schuttle Avenue, and the Sierra Cinnabar Grant, Schuttle Square, all of which addresses will reach me at my little old desk-room corner in 1126 Tremont Building, Third and Schuttle Avenues; and I'll answer letters of inquiry on four different letter-heads. If you need more I'll post Billy Riggs over in the Cloud Block and fix it for another four or five."

"I'll write Billy a letter myself," observed J. Rufus. "I'll need all the references I can get when I come to organize the Universal Covered Carpet Tack Company."

"Quit kidding," retorted Mr. Daw.

"It's on the level," insisted J. Rufus seriously. "Let's go down to dinner."

Chapter 2

Wherein Edward Lamb Beholds the Amazing Profits of the
Carpet Tack Industry

There were twenty-four applicants for the position before Edward Lamb appeared, the second day after the initial insertion of the advertisement which had been designed to meet his eye alone. David Jasper, who read his paper advertisements and all, in order to get the full worth of his money out of it, telephoned to his friend Edward about the glittering chance.

Yes, Mr. Wallingford was in his suite. Would the gentleman give his name? Mr. Lamb produced a card, printed in careful imitation of engraving, and it gained him admission to the August presence, where he created some surprise by a sudden burst of laughter.

"Ex-cuse me!" he exclaimed. "But you're the man that splashed mud on me the other night!"

When the circumstance was related, Mr. Wallingford laughed with great gusto and shook hands for the second time with his visitor. The incident helped them to get upon a most cordial footing at once. It did not occur to either of them, at the time, how appropriate it was that Mr. Wallingford should splash mud upon Mr. Lamb at their very first meeting.

"What can I do for you, Mr. Lamb?" inquired the large man.

"You advertised—" began the caller.

"Oh, you came about that position," deprecated Mr. Wallingford, with a nicely shaded tone of courteous disappointment in his voice. "I am afraid that I am already fairly well suited, although I have made no final choice as yet. What are your qualifications?"

"There will be no trouble about that," returned Mr. Lamb, straightening visibly. "I can satisfy anybody." And Mr. Wallingford had the keynote for which he was seeking.

He knew at once that Mr. Lamb prided himself upon his independence, upon his local standing, upon his efficiency, upon his business astuteness. The observer had also the experience of Mr. Daw to guide him, and, moreover, better than all, here was Mr. Lamb himself. He was a broad-shouldered young man, who stood well upon his two feet; he dressed with a proper and decent pride in his prosperity, and wore looped upon his vest a watch chain that by its very weight bespoke the wearer's solid worth. The young man was an open book, whereof the pages were embossed in large type.

"Now you're talking like the right man," said the prospective employer. "Sit down. You'll understand, Mr. Lamb, that my question was only a natural one, for I am quite particular about this position, which is the most important one I have to fill. Our business is to be a large one. We are to conduct an immense plant in this city, and I want the office work organized with a thorough system from the beginning. The duties, consequently, would begin at once. The man who would become secretary of the Universal Covered Carpet Tack Company, would need to know all about the concern from its very inception, and until I have secured that exact man I shall take no steps toward organization."

Word by word, Mr. Wallingford watched the face of Edward Lamb and could see that he was succumbing to the mental chloroform. However, a man who at thirty has accumulated five thousand is not apt to be numbed without struggling.

"Before we go any further," interposed the patient, with deep, deep shrewdness, "it must be understood that I have no money to invest."

"Exactly," agreed Mr. Wallingford. "I stated that in my advertisement. To become secretary it will be necessary to hold one share of stock, but that share I shall give to the right applicant. I do not care for him to have any investment in the company. What I want is the services of the best man in the city, and to that end I advertised for one who had been an expert bookkeeper and who knew all the office routine of conducting a large business, agreeing to start such a man with a salary of two hundred dollars a month. That advertisement stated in full all that I expect from the one who secures this position—his expert services. I may say that you are only the second candidate who has had the outward appearance of being able to fulfill the requirements. Actual efficiency would naturally have to be shown."

Mr. Wallingford was now quite coldly insistent. The proper sleep had been induced.

"For fifteen years," Mr. Lamb now hastened to advise him, "I have been employed by the A. J. Dorman Manufacturing Company, and can refer you to them for everything you wish to know. I can give you other references as to reliability if you like."

Mr. Wallingford was instant warmth.

"The A. J. Dorman Company, indeed!" he exclaimed, though he had never heard of that concern. "The name itself is guarantee enough, at least to defer such matters for a bit while I show you the industry that is to be built in your city." From his dresser Mr. Wallingford produced a handful of tacks, the head of each one covered with a bit of different colored bright cloth. "You have only to look at these," he continued, holding them forth, and with the thumb and forefinger of the other hand turning one red-topped tack about in front of Mr. Lamb's eyes, "to appreciate to the full what a wonderful business certainty I am preparing to launch. Just hold these tacks a moment," and he turned the handful into Mr. Lamb's outstretched palm. "Now come over to the edge of this carpet. I have selected here a tack which matches this floor covering. You see those rusty heads? Imagine the difference if they were replaced by this!''

Mr. Lamb looked and saw; but it was necessary to display his business acumen.

"Looks like a good thing," he commented; "but the cost?"

"The cost is comparatively nothing over the old steel tack, although we can easily get ten cents a paper as against five for the common ones, leaving us a much wider margin of profit than the manufacturers of the straight tack obtain. There is no family so poor that will use the old, rusty tinned or bronze tack when these are made known to the trade, and you can easily compute for yourself how many millions of packages are used every year. Why, the Eureka Tack Company, which practically has a monopoly of the carpet-tack business, operates a manufacturing plant covering twenty solid acres, and a loaded freight car leaves its warehouse doors on an average of every seven minutes! You cannot buy a share of stock in the Eureka Carpet Tack Company at any price. It yields sixteen per cent a year dividends, with over eighteen million dollars of undivided surplus—and that business was built on carpet tacks alone! Why, sir, if we wished to do so, within two months after we had started our factory wheels rolling we could sell out to the Eureka Company for two million dollars; or a profit of more than one thousand per cent on the investment that we are to make.''

For once Mr. Lamb was overwhelmed. Only three days before he had been beset by Mr. Daw, but that gentleman had grown hoarsely eloquent over vast possessions that were beyond thousands of miles of circumambient space across vast barren reaches where desert sands sent up constant streams of superheated atmosphere, with the ''hot air'' distinctly to be traced throughout the conversation; but here was something to be seen and felt. The points of the very tacks that he held pricked his palm, and his eyes were still glued upon the red-topped one which Mr. Wallingford held hypnotically before him.

"Who composes your company?" he managed to ask.

"So far, I do," replied Mr. Wallingford with quiet pride. "I have not organized the company. That is a minor detail. When I go searching for capital I shall know where to secure it. I have chosen this city on account of its manufacturing facilities, and for its splendid geographical position as a distributing center.''

"The stock is not yet placed, then," mused aloud Mr. Lamb, upon whose vision there already glowed a pleasing picture of immense profits.

Why, the thing was startling in the magnificence of its opportunity! Simple little trick, millions and millions used, better than anything of its kind ever put upon the market, cheaply manufactured, it was marked for success from the first!

"Stock placed? Not at all," stated Mr. Wallingford. "My plans only contemplate incorporating for a quarter of a million, and I mean to avoid small stockholders. I shall try to divide the stock into, say, about ten holdings of twenty-five thousand each."

Mr. Lamb was visibly disappointed.

"It looks like a fine thing," he declared with a note of regret.

"Fine? My boy, I'm not much older than you are, but I have been connected with several large enterprises in Boston and elsewhere—if any one were to care to inquire about me they might drop a line to the Mexican and Rio Grande Rubber Company, the St. John's Blood Orange Plantation Company, the Los Pocos Lead Development Company, the Sierra Cinnabar Grant, and a number of others, the addresses of which I could supply—and I never have seen anything so good as this. I am staking my entire business judgment upon it, and, of course, I shall retain the majority of stock myself, inasmuch as the article is my invention."

This being the psychological moment, Mr. Wallingford put forth his hand and had Mr. Lamb dump the tacks back into the large palm that had at first held them. He left them open to view, however, and presently Mr. Lamb picked out one of them for examination. This particular tack was of an exquisite apple-green color, the covering for which had been clipped from one of Mr. Wallingford's own expensive ties, glued to its place and carefully trimmed by Mr. Wallingford's own hands. Mr. Lamb took it to the window for closer admiration, and the promoter, left to himself for a moment, stood before the glass to mop his face and head and neck. He had been working until he had perspired; but, looking into the glass at Mr. Lamb's rigid back, he perceived that the work was well done. Mr. Lamb was profoundly convinced that the Universal Covered Carpet Tack Company was an entity to be respected; nay, to be revered! Mr. Lamb could already see the smoke belching from the tall chimneys of its factory, the bright lights gleaming out from its myriad windows where it was working overtime, the thousands of workmen streaming in at its broad gates, the loaded freight cars leaving every seven minutes!

"You're not going home to dinner, are you, Mr. Lamb?" asked Mr. Wallingford suddenly.

"I owe you one for the splash, you know."

"Why—I'm expected home."

"Telephone them you're not coming."

"We—we haven't a telephone in the house."

"Telephone to the nearest drug store and send a messenger over."

Mr. Lamb looked down at himself. He was always neatly dressed, but he did not feel equal to the glitter of the big dining room downstairs.

"I am not—cleaned up," he objected.

"Nonsense! However, as far as that goes, we'll have 'em bring a table right here." And taking the matter into his own hands, Mr. Wallingford telephoned for a waiter.

From that moment Mr. Lamb strove not to show his wonder at the heights to which human comfort and luxury can attain, but it was a vain attempt; for from the time the two uniformed attendants brought in the table with its snowy cloth and began to place upon it the shining silver and cut-glass service, with the centerpiece of red carnations, he began to grasp at the new world—and it was about this time that he wished he had on his best black suit. In the bathroom Mr. Wallingford came upon him as he held his collar ruefully in his hand, and needed no explanation.

"I say, old man, we can't keep 'em clean, can we? We'll fix that."

The bellboys were anxious to answer summons from 44-A by this time. Mr. Wallingford never used money in a hotel except for tips. It was scarcely a minute until a boy had that collar, with instructions to get another just like it.

"How are the cuffs? Attached, old man? All right. What size shirt do you wear?"

Mr. Lamb gave up. He was now past the point of protest. He told Mr. Wallingford the number of his shirt. In five minutes more he was completely outfitted with clean linen, and when, washed and refreshed and spotless as to high lights, he stepped forth into what was now a perfectly appointed private dining room, he felt himself gradually rising to Mr. Wallingford's own height and able to be supercilious to the waiters, under whose gaze, while his collar was soiled, he had quailed.

It was said by those who made a business of dining that Mr. Wallingford could order a dinner worth while, except for the one trifling fault of over-plenty; but then, Mr. Wallingford himself was a large man, and it took much food and drink to sustain that largeness. Whatever other critics might have said, Mr. Lamb could have but one opinion as they sipped their champagne, toward the end of the meal, and this opinion was that Mr. Wallingford was a genius, a prince of entertainers, a master of finance, a gentleman to be imitated in every particular, and that a man should especially blush to question his financial standing or integrity.

They went to the theater after dinner—box seats—and after the theater they had a little cold snack, amounting to about eleven dollars, including wine and cigars. Moreover, Mr. Lamb had gratefully accepted the secretaryship of the Universal Covered Carpet Tack Company.

New York: A. L. Burt Co.

STUDY QUESTIONS

1. To what extent does Wright seem to recognize that the "liberty" and "equality" Jefferson talks about are not compatible concepts?

2. Jefferson had white males in mind when he wrote the Declaration of Independence. Who was Wright thinking about when he wrote *Black Boy*?

3. From Wright's perspective, could the Declaration of Independence do for African Americans what Jefferson proposed it should do for European Americans?

4. How does Crèvecoeur's notion of what an American is compare to Wright's in *Black Boy*?

5. What groups do neither Crèvecoeur nor Wright seem to have in mind when they define "American"?

6. What would Wright and Crèvecoeur regard as success?

7. Why was the South not able to destroy Wright's dream of success?

8. Why did white men not want to hear any talk about the Thirteenth, Fourteenth, and Fifteenth Amendments to the Constitution in front of black people?

9. Are these amendments honored now?

10. Why did Wright not just abandon his dream of success?

11. Are there any parallels between Wallingford and the young Richard Wright?

12. How important is money to Wallingford and to Wright?

13. For what particular purpose did Wright want to make money quickly?

14. How does Wright's version of the American dream differ from Wallingford's?

TOPICS FOR WRITTEN OR ORAL EXPLORATION

1. Even with all the obstacles Wright had to face, he retained his belief in some version of the American dream of success. How would you account for this, based on what he reveals in *Black Boy*?

2. Write a paper in which you list and account for the differences between the American dream of success as defined in the documents in this chapter and the black community's dreams of success in *Black Boy*.

3. Did Wright realize his version of the dream? Why or why not?

4. What would you have done differently if you had been in Wright's circumstances, and if you had been determined to realize your version of the American dream? Account for the differences.

5. Why has the competition for making the dream come true been restricted, until recently, to white males? If the competition is opened up to everyone, will the increased opportunity mean that more or fewer people will succeed?

6. If Wright had been white, and he had tried to achieve the American dream, do you think it would have been as a writer? Why or why not?

7. After reading *Black Boy*, how certain are you that you can achieve the American dream? How much and in what ways have racial conditions in this country changed since Wright's childhood?

8. Is Wright trying to suggest in *Black Boy* that the American dream of success needs to be redefined? Defend your answer in an essay based on evidence from the book.

9. What do you think "success" is? What do you think it should be based on? To what extent do your answers match Wright's in *Black Boy*?

10. What is your family's relationship to the American dream? Your own relationship to it?

11. Divide the class into teams representing different answers to the question of what constitutes success, and then have the teams debate who has the most compelling definition.

12. Does our society believe, as Andrew Carnegie once suggested, that the greatest glory to God is a multimillionaire?

SUGGESTED READINGS

See the complete texts of *Letters from an American Farmer* and *Get-Rich-Quick Wallingford*. Also examine treatments of the American dream by F. Scott Fitzgerald (especially *The Great Gatsby*); Thomas Wolfe; Theodore Dreiser (especially *An American Tragedy*); John Steinbeck (particularly *The Grapes of Wrath*); Edward Albee, *The American Dream*; Norman Mailer, *An American Dream*; and Horatio Alger, Jr., *Struggling Upward and Other Works*.

4

The Dream Deferred

As Wright knew all too well, and as African Americans learned all too quickly, the end of the Civil War in 1865 did not mean the end of slavery; racially speaking, the South won the war. The high expectations in the black community met a reality that was in many ways worse than legal slavery. Law and custom quickly reestablished the racial status quo after Reconstruction ended in 1877. Blacks were then on their own, left to fight a social system that was fundamentally feudalistic and extremely hierarchical, a system in which no matter how capable or decent a human being you were, unless you were white, male, heterosexual, Protestant, and well off, you were at a profound disadvantage. Ultimately, the system required and still requires a minority to hate and despise to keep it going. Wright found it intolerable.

Neither Wright, as he so powerfully says in *Black Boy*, nor other African Americans accepted the idea that the dream of racial equality would have to be permanently deferred. On the contrary, they used every means at their disposal to bring the dream closer to reality. Booker T. Washington and W.E.B. Du Bois both used what may be seen as interrelated ways of improving the condition of black Americans after Reconstruction. In their different ways, they attacked the racism that Wright was so indignant toward in his autobiography. More outspoken than Washington and Du Bois,

Wright was nevertheless indebted to them for initiating a conversation that is still very loud today, a conversation between varying degrees of accommodation, on the one hand, and militancy, on the other.

REACTION

When the Civil War ended in 1865, white Southerners moved quickly on many fronts to hold on to the advantages they had enjoyed when slavery was legal. One way they did this was through the legal system; as *Black Boy* reveals, Wright frequently felt the pressure of laws that told him whom he could not marry, where he had to sit on the train, who, in fact, he was. These laws, termed Black Codes, were used to maintain the racial status quo during Reconstruction; Jim Crow and provisions contained in state constitutions were used to maintain it after Reconstruction ended in 1877.

FROM THE NORTH CAROLINA "BLACK CODE" (1866)

Sec. I. *Be it enacted by the General Assembly of the State of North Carolina.* . . . That negroes and their issue, even where one ancestor in each succeeding generation to the fourth inclusive is white, shall be deemed persons of color.

Public Laws of North Carolina, session of 1866, p. 99; and Senate Ex. Doc. No. 26, 39 Cong., 1 Sess., p. 197. [March 10, 1866]

FROM MISSISSIPPI'S "JIM CROW" LAWS (1865)

[November 21, 1865]

Sec. 3 . . . All freedmen, free negroes or mulattoes who do now and have herebefore lived and cohabited together as husband and wife shall be taken and held in law as legally married, and the issue shall be taken and held as legitimate for all purposes; that it shall not be lawful for any freedman, free negro, or mulatto to intermarry with any white person; nor for any white person to intermarry with any freedman, free negro, or mulatto; and any person who shall so intermarry, shall be deemed guilty of felony, and on conviction thereof shall be confined in the State penitentiary for life; and those shall be deemed freedman, free negroes, and mulattoes who are of pure negro blood, and those descended from a negro to the third generation, inclusive, though one ancestor in each generation may have been a white person.

Sec. 6. It shall be unlawful for any officer, station agent, collector, or employee on any railroad in this State, to allow any freedman, negro, or mulatto, to ride in any first class passenger cars, set apart, or used by, and for white persons; and any person offending against the provisions of this section, shall be deemed guilty of a misdemeanor; and on conviction thereof before the circuit court of the county in which said offence was committed, shall be fined not less than fifty dollars, nor more than five hundred dollars; and shall be imprisoned in the county jail, until such fine, and costs of prosecution are paid: *Provided*, That this section of this act, shall not apply, in the case of negroes or mulattoes, traveling with their mistress, in the capacity of maids.

Laws of Mississippi, 1865, pp. 82, 231.

FROM THE CONSTITUTION OF THE STATE OF MISSISSIPPI (1890)

Section 263. The marriage of a white person with a negro or mulatto, or person who shall have one-eighth or more of negro blood, shall be unlawful and void.

CAST DOWN YOUR BUCKET WHERE YOU ARE

Up from Slavery, Booker T. Washington's autobiography, was published just a few years before Wright was born. Its narrator argues
that the most useful strategy for African Americans is to make the
best of the status quo, a doctrine Wright found repulsive and impossible to accept. Washington lies to and flatters his white readers
to build up his own power and to secure their financial support
for Tuskegee Institute. In telling former slaves and their descendants to cast down their buckets where they are, Washington is
trying to reassure whites, while getting blacks on the first rung of
the social ladder. Such gradualist politics is completely unconge-
nial to Wright's sensibility, but then Wright was not interested in
personal power or in establishing a black college. Washington complicated the task of his successors in the African American autobiographical tradition by wearing a mask that may have deceived the
observer, the wearer, or both.

FROM BOOKER T. WASHINGTON, *UP FROM SLAVERY* (1901)

Chapter 14

The Atlanta Exposition Address

The Atlanta Exposition, at which I had been asked to make an address
as a representative of the Negro race . . . was opened with a short address
from Governor Bullock. After other interesting exercises, including an
invocation from Bishop Nelson, of Georgia, a dedicatory ode by Albert
Howell, Jr., and addresses by the President of the Exposition and Mrs.
Joseph Thompson, the President of the Woman's Board, Governor Bullock introduced me with the words, "We have with us to-day a representative of Negro enterprise and Negro civilization."

When I arose to speak, there was considerable cheering, especially
from the coloured people. As I remember it now, the thing that was
uppermost in my mind was the desire to say something that would cement the friendship of the races and bring about hearty cooperation between them. So far as my outward surroundings were concerned, the
only thing that I recall distinctly now is that when I got up, I saw

thousands of eyes looking intently into my face. The following is the address which I delivered:—

MR. PRESIDENT AND GENTLEMEN OF THE BOARD OF DIRECTORS AND CITIZENS.

One-third of the population in the South is of the Negro race. No enterprise seeking the material, civil, or moral welfare of this section can disregard this element of our population and reach the highest success. I but convey to you, Mr. President and Directors, the sentiment of the masses of my race when I say that in no way have the value and manhood of the American Negro been more fittingly and generously recognized than by the managers of this magnificent Exposition at every stage of its progress. It is a recognition that will do more to cement the friendship of the two races than any occurrence since the dawn of our freedom.

Not only this, but the opportunity here afforded will awaken among us a new era of industrial progress. Ignorant and inexperienced, it is not strange that in the first years of our new life we began at the top instead of at the bottom; that a seat in Congress or the state legislature was more sought than real estate or industrial skill; that the political convention of stump speaking had more attractions than starting a dairy farm or truck garden.

A ship lost at sea for many days suddenly sighted a friendly vessel. From the mast of the unfortunate vessel was seen a signal, "Water, water; we die of thirst!" The answer from the friendly vessel at once came back, "Cast down your bucket where you are." A second time the signal, "Water, water; send us water!" ran up from the distressed vessel, and was answered, "Cast down your bucket where you are." And a third and fourth signal for water was answered, "Cast down your bucket where you are." The captain of the distressed vessel, at last heeding the injunction, cast down his bucket, and it came up full of fresh, sparkling water from the mouth of the Amazon River. To those of my race who depend on bettering their condition in a foreign land or who underestimate the importance of cultivating friendly relations with the Southern white man, who is their next-door neighbour, I would say: "Cast down your bucket where you are"—cast it down in making friends in every manly way of the people of all races by whom we are surrounded.

Cast it down in agriculture, mechanics, in commerce, in domestic service, and in the professions. And in this connection it is well to bear in mind that whatever other sins the South may be called to bear, when it comes to business, pure and simple, it is in the South that the Negro is given a man's chance in the commercial world, and in nothing is this Exposition more eloquent than in emphasizing this chance. Our greatest danger is that in the great leap from slavery to freedom we may overlook the fact that the masses of us are to live by the productions of our hands, and fail to keep in mind that we shall prosper in proportion as we learn to dignify and glorify common labour and put brains and skill into the common occupations of life; shall prosper in proportion as we learn to draw the line between the superficial and the substantial, the ornamental gewgaws of life and the useful. No race can prosper till it learns that there is as much dignity in tilling a field as in writing a poem. It is at the bottom of life we must begin, and not at the top. Nor should we permit our grievances to overshadow our opportunities.

To those of the white race who look to the incoming of those of foreign birth and strange tongue and habits for the prosperity of the South, were I permitted I would repeat what I say to my own race, "Cast down your bucket where you are." Cast it down among the eight millions of Negroes whose habits you know, whose fidelity and love you have tested in days when to have proved treacherous meant the ruin of your firesides. Cast down your bucket among these people who have, without strikes and labour wars, tilled your fields, cleared your forests, builded your railroads and cities, and brought forth treasures from the bowels of the earth, and helped make possible this magnificent representation of the progress of the South. Casting down your bucket among my people, helping and encouraging them as you are doing on these grounds, and to education of head, hand, and heart, you will find that they will buy your surplus land, make blossom the waste places in your fields, and run your factories. While doing this, you can be sure in the future, as in the past, that you and your families will be surrounded by the most patient, faithful, law-abiding, and unresentful people that the world has seen. As we have proved our loyalty to you in the past, in nursing your children, watching by the sick-bed of your mothers and fathers, and often following them with tear-dimmed eyes to their graves, so in the future, in our humble way, we shall stand by you with a devotion that no foreigner can approach, ready to lay down our lives, if need be, in defence of yours, interlacing our industrial, commercial, civil, and religious life with yours in a way that shall make the interests of both races one. In all things that are purely social we can be as separate as the fingers, yet one as the hand in all things essential to mutual progress.

There is no defence or security for any of us except in the highest intelligence and development of all. If anywhere there are efforts tending to curtail the fullest growth of the Negro, let these efforts be turned into stimulating, encouraging, and making him the most useful and intelligent citizen. Effort or means so invested will pay a thousand per cent interest. These efforts will be twice blessed—"blessing him that gives and him that takes."

There is no escape through law of man or God from the inevitable:—

> The laws of changeless justice bind
>   Oppressor with oppressed;
> And close as sin and suffering joined
>   We march to fate abreast.

Nearly sixteen millions of hands will aid you in pulling the load upward, or they will pull against you the load downward. We shall constitute one-third and more of the ignorance and crime of the South, or one-third its intelligence and progress; we shall contribute one-third to the business and industrial prosperity of the South, or we shall prove a veritable body of death, stagnating, depressing, retarding every effort to advance the body politic.

Gentlemen of the Exposition, as we present to you our humble effort at an exhibition of our progress, you must not expect overmuch. Starting thirty years ago with ownership here and there in a few quilts and pumpkins and chickens (gathered from miscellaneous sources), remember the path that has led from these to the inventions and production of agricultural implements, buggies, steam-engines, newspapers, books, statuary, carving, paintings, the management of drug-stores and banks, has not been trodden without contact with thorns and thistles. While we take pride in what we exhibit as a result of our independent efforts, we do not for a moment forget that our part in this exhibition would fall far short of your expectations but for the constant help that has come to our educational life, not only from the Southern states, but especially from Northern philanthropists, who have made their gifts a constant stream of blessing and encouragement.

The wisest among my race understand that the agitation of questions of social equality is the extremest folly, and that progress in the enjoyment of all the privileges that will come to us must be the result of severe and constant struggle rather than of artificial forcing. No race that has anything to contribute to the markets of the world is long in any degree ostracized. It is important and right that all privileges of the law be ours, but it is vastly more important that we be prepared for the exercises of these privileges. The opportunity to earn a dollar in a factory just now is worth infinitely more than the opportunity to spend a dollar in an opera-house.

In conclusion, may I repeat that nothing in thirty years has given us more hope and encouragement, and drawn us so near to you of the white race, as this opportunity offered by the Exposition; and here bending, as it were, over the altar that represents the result of the struggles of your race and mine, both starting practically empty-handed three decades ago. I pledge that in your effort to work out the great and intricate problem which God has laid at the doors of the South, you shall have at all times the patient, sympathetic help of my race; only let this be constantly in sociation and every conference or religious body of any kind, of my race, that met, did not fail before adjourning to pass a resolution condemning me, or calling upon me to retract or modify what I had said. Many of these organizations went so far in their resolutions as to advise parents to cease sending their children to Tuskegee. One association even appointed a "missionary" whose duty it was to warn the people against sending their children to Tuskegee. The missionary had a son in the school, and I noticed that, whatever the "missionary" might have said or done with regard to others, he was careful not to take his son away from the institution. Many of the coloured papers, especially those that were the organs of religious bodies, joined in the general chorus of condemnation or demands for retraction.

During the whole time of the excitement, and through all the criticism, I did not utter a word of explanation or retraction. I knew that I was right, and that time and the sober second thought of the people would vindicate me. It was not long before the bishops and other church leaders began to make a careful investigation of the conditions of the ministry, and they found out that I was right. In fact, the oldest and most influential bishop in one branch of the Methodist Church said that my words were far too mild. Very soon public sentiment began making itself felt, in demanding a purifying of the ministry. While this is not yet complete by any means, I think I may say, without egotism, and I have been told by many of our most influential ministers, that my words had much to do with starting a demand for the placing of a higher type of men in the pulpit. I have had the satisfaction of having many who once condemned me thank me heartily for my frank words.

The change of the attitude of the Negro ministry, so far as regards myself, is so complete that at the present time I have no warmer friends among any class than I have among the clergymen. The improvement in the character and life of the Negro ministers is one of the most gratifying evidences of the progress of the race. My experience with them, as well as other events in my life, convince me that the thing to do, when one feels sure that he has said or done the right thing, and is condemned, is to stand still and keep quiet. If he is right, time will show it.

In the midst of the discussion which was going on concerning my Atlanta speech, I received the letter which I give below, from Dr. Gilman, the President of Johns Hopkins University, who had been made chairman of the judges of award in connection with the Atlanta Exposition:—

JOHNS HOPKINS UNIVERSITY, BALTIMORE,
President's Office, September 30, 1895.

DEAR MR. WASHINGTON: Would it be agreeable to you to be one of the Judges of Award in the Department of Education at Atlanta?

mind, that, while from representations in these buildings of the product of field, of forest, of mine, of factory, letters, and art, much good will come, yet far above and beyond material benefits will be that higher good, that, let us pray God, will come, in a blotting out of sectional differences and racial animosities and suspicions, in a determination to administer absolute justice, in a willing obedience among all classes to the mandates of law. This, then, coupled with our material prosperity, will bring into our beloved South a new heaven and a new earth.

The first thing that I remember, after I had finished speaking, was that Governor Bullock rushed across the platform and took me by the hand, and that others did the same. I received so many and such hearty congratulations that I found it difficult to get out of the building. I did not appreciate to any degree, however, the impression which my address seemed to have made, until the next morning, when I went into the business part of the city. As soon as I was recognized, I was surprised to find myself pointed out and surrounded by a crowd of men who wished to shake hands with me. This was kept up on every street on to which I went, to an extent which embarrassed me so much that I went back to my boarding place. The next morning I returned to Tuskegee. At the station in Atlanta, and at almost all of the stations at which the train stopped between that city and Tuskegee, I found a crowd of people anxious to shake hands with me.

The papers in all parts of the United States published the address in full, and for months afterward there were complimentary editorial references to it. Mr. Clark Howell, the editor of the Atlanta *Constitution*, telegraphed to a New York paper, among other words, the following, "I do not exaggerate when I say that Professor Booker T. Washington's address yesterday was one of the most notable speeches, both as to character and as to the warmth of its reception, ever delivered to a Southern audience. The address was a revelation. The whole speech is a platform upon which blacks and whites can stand with full justice to each other."

The Boston *Transcript* said editorially: "The speech of Booker T. Washington at the Atlanta Exposition, this week, seems to have dwarfed all the other proceedings and the Exposition itself. The sensation that it has caused in the press has never been equalled."

I very soon began receiving all kinds of propositions from lecture bureaus, and editors of magazines and papers, to take the lecture platform, and to write articles. One lecture bureau offered me fifty thousand dollars, or two hundred dollars a night and expenses, if I would place my services at its disposal for a given period. To all these communications I replied that my life-work was at Tuskegee; and that whenever I spoke it must be in the interests of the Tuskegee school and my race, and that

I would enter into no arrangements that seemed to place a mere commercial value upon my services.

Some days after its delivery I sent a copy of my address to the President of the United States, the Hon. Grover Cleveland. I received from him the following autographed reply:—

GRAY GABLES, BUZZARD'S BAY, MASS.,
OCTOBER 6, 1895

BOOKER T. WASHINGTON, ESQ.:

MY DEAR SIR: I thank you for sending me a copy of your address delivered at the Atlanta Exposition.

I thank you with much enthusiasm for making the address. I have read it with intense interest, and I think the Exposition would be fully justified if it did not do more than furnish the opportunity for its delivery. Your words cannot fail to delight and encourage all who wish well for your race; and if our coloured fellow-citizens do not from your utterances gather new hope and form new determinations to gain every valuable advantage offered them by their citizenship, it will be strange indeed.

Yours very truly,
GROVER CLEVELAND.

Later I met Mr. Cleveland, for the first time, when, as President, he visited the Atlanta Exposition. At the request of myself and others he consented to spend an hour in the Negro Building, for the purpose of inspecting the Negro exhibit and of giving the coloured people in attendance an opportunity to shake hands with him. As soon as I met Mr. Cleveland I became impressed with his simplicity, greatness, and rugged honesty. I have met him many times since then, both at public functions and at his private residence in Princeton, and the more I see of him the more I admire him. When he visited the Negro Building in Atlanta he seemed to give himself up wholly, for that hour, to the coloured people. He seemed to be as careful to shake hands with some old coloured "auntie" clad partially in rags, and to take as much pleasure in doing so, as if he were greeting some millionnaire. Many of the coloured people took advantage of the occasion to get him to write his name in a book or on a slip of paper. He was as careful and patient in doing this as if he were putting his signature to some great state document.

Mr. Cleveland has not only shown his friendship for me in many personal ways, but has always consented to do anything I have asked of him for our school. This he has done, whether it was to make a personal

donation or to use his influence in securing the donations of others. Judging from my personal acquaintance with Mr. Cleveland, I do not believe that he is conscious of possessing any colour prejudice. He is too great for that. In my contact with people I find that, as a rule, it is only the little, narrow people who live for themselves, who never read good books, who do not travel, who never open up their souls in a way to permit them to come into contact with other souls—with the great outside world. No man whose vision is bounded by colour can come into contact with what is highest and best in the world. In meeting men, in many places, I have found that the happiest people are those who do the most for others; the most miserable are those who do the least. I have also found that few things, if any, are capable of making one so blind and narrow as race prejudice. I often say to our students, in the course of my talks to them on Sunday evenings in the chapel, that the longer I live and the more experience I have of the world, the more I am convinced that, after all, the one thing that is most worth living for—and dying for, if need be—is the opportunity of making some one else more happy and more useful.

The coloured people and the coloured newspapers at first seemed to be greatly pleased with the character of my Atlanta address, as well as with its reception. But after the first burst of enthusiasm began to die away, and the coloured people began reading the speech in cold type, some of them seemed to feel that they had been hypnotized. They seemed to feel that I had been too liberal in my remarks toward the Southern whites, and that I had not spoken out strongly enough for what they termed the "rights" of the race. For a while there was a reaction, so far as a certain element of my own race was concerned, but later these reactionary ones seemed to have been won over to my way of believing and acting.

While speaking of changes in public sentiment, I recall that about ten years after the school at Tuskegee was established, I had an experience that I shall never forget. Dr. Lyman Abbott, then the pastor of Plymouth Church, and also editor of the *Outlook* (then the *Christian Union*), asked me to write a letter for his paper giving my opinion of the exact condition, mental and moral, of the coloured ministers in the South, as based upon my observations. I wrote the letter, giving the exact facts as I conceived them to be. The picture painted was a rather black one—or, since I am black, shall I say "white"? It could not be otherwise with a race but a few years out of slavery, a race which had not had time or opportunity to produce a competent ministry.

What I said soon reached every Negro minister in the country, I think, and the letters of condemnation which I received from them were not few. I think that for a year after the publication of this article every as-

If so, I shall be glad to place your name upon the list. A line by telegraph will be welcomed.

Yours very truly,
D. C. GILMAN.

I think I was even more surprised to receive this invitation than I had been to receive the invitation to speak at the opening of the Exposition. It was to be a part of my duty, as one of the jurors, to pass not only upon the exhibits of the coloured schools, but also upon those of the white schools. I accepted the position, and spent a month in Atlanta in performance of the duties which it entailed. The board of jurors was a large one, consisting in all of sixty members. It was about equally divided between Southern white people and Northern white people. Among them were college presidents, leading scientists and men of letters, and specialists in many subjects. When the group of jurors to which I was assigned met for organization, Mr. Thomas Nelson Page, who was one of the number, moved that I be made secretary of that division, and the motion was unanimously adopted. Nearly half of our division were Southern people. In performing my duties in the inspection of the exhibits of white schools I was in every case treated with respect, and at the close of our labours I parted from my associates with regret.

I am often asked to express myself more freely than I do upon the political condition and the political future of my race. These recollections of my experience in Atlanta give me the opportunity to do so briefly. My own belief is, although I have never before said so in so many words, that the time will come when the Negro in the South will be accorded all the political rights which his ability, character, and material possessions entitle him to. I think, though, that the opportunity to freely exercise such political rights will not come in any large degree through outside or artificial forcing, but will be accorded to the Negro by the Southern white people themselves, and that they will protect him in the exercise of those rights. Just as soon as the South gets over the old feeling that it is being forced by "foreigners," or "aliens," to do something which it does not want to do, I believe that the change in the direction that I have indicated is going to begin. In fact, there are indications that it is already beginning in a slight degree.

Let me illustrate my meaning. Suppose that some months before the opening of the Atlanta Exposition there had been a general demand from the press and public platform outside the South that a Negro be given a place on the opening programme, and that a Negro be placed upon the board of jurors of award. Would any such recognition of the race have taken place? I do not think so. The Atlanta officials went as far as they did because they felt it to be a pleasure, as well as a duty, to reward what they considered merit in the Negro race. Say what we will, there is something in human nature which we cannot blot out, which makes one man, in the end, recognize and reward merit in another, regardless of colour or race.

I believe it is the duty of the Negro—as the greater part of the race is already doing—to deport himself modestly in regard to political claims, depending upon the slow but sure influences that proceed from the possession of property, intelligence, and high character for the full recognition of his political rights. I think that the according of the full exercise of political rights is going to be a matter of natural, slow growth, not an over-night, gourd-vine affair. I do not believe that the Negro should cease voting, for a man cannot learn the exercise of self-government by ceasing to vote any more than a boy can learn to swim by keeping out of the water, but I do believe that in this voting he should more and more be influenced by those of intelligence and character who are his next-door neighbours.

I know coloured men who, through the encouragement, help, and advice of Southern white people, have accumulated thousands of dollars' worth of property, but who, at the same time, would never think of going to those same persons for advice concerning the casting of their ballots. This, it seems to me, is unwise and unreasonable, and should cease. In saying this I do not mean that the Negro should truckle, or not vote from principle, for the instant he ceases to vote from principle he loses the confidence and respect of the Southern white man even.

I do not believe that any state should make a law that permits an ignorant and poverty-stricken white man to vote, and prevents a black man in the same condition from voting. Such a law is not only unjust, but it will react, as all unjust laws do, in time; for the effect of such a law is to encourage the Negro to secure education and property, and at the same time it encourages the white man to remain in ignorance and poverty. I believe that in time, through the operation of intelligence and friendly race relations, all cheating at the ballot box in the South will cease. It will become apparent that the white man who begins by cheating a Negro out of his ballot soon learns to cheat a white man out of his, and that the man who does this ends his career of dishonesty by the theft of property or by some equally serious crime. In my opinion, the time will come when the South will encourage all of its citizens to vote. It will see that it pays better, from every standpoint, to have healthy, vigorous life than to have that political stagnation which always results when one-half of the population has no share and no interest in the Government.

As a rule, I believe in universal, free suffrage, but I believe that in the South we are confronted with peculiar conditions that justify the protection of the ballot in many of the states, for a while at least, either by an educational test, a property test, or by both combined; but whatever tests are required, they should be made to apply with equal and exact justice to both races.

New York: Doubleday, Page and Co.

RECONSTRUCTION

To counter the racist distortions, falsifications, self-justifying myths, and romantic indulgence that came to dominate the consciousness of many white Americans about African Americans, even more after the Civil War than before it, W.E.B. Du Bois wrote *The Souls of Black Folk*. The degree to which his efforts to set the record straight were unsuccessful can be determined with considerable confidence by realizing that two films, *The Birth of a Nation* (1915) and *Gone with the Wind* (1939), are still taken as accurate depictions of the Reconstruction period even now, when one might expect that such pernicious racist fantasies would be recognized by every American. In the excerpt reprinted here, Du Bois makes clear how complicated and difficult life was for blacks after the Civil War. He also makes clear how ridiculous it is to blame them for the South's problems, because they still had very little power. Although historians have sometimes faulted Du Bois's lack of documentation, his essential point holds: blacks were victims during Reconstruction; conceiving of them otherwise is merely a pretext for treating them the way Wright was treated as he grew up.

FROM W.E.B. DU BOIS, *THE SOULS OF BLACK FOLK* (1903)

Chapter 2

The problem of the twentieth century is the problem of the color-line,— the relation of the darker to the lighter races of men in Asia and Africa, in America and the islands of the sea. It was a phase of this problem that caused the Civil War; and however much they who marched South and North in 1861 may have fixed on the technical points of union and local autonomy as a shibboleth, all nevertheless knew, as we know, that the question of Negro slavery was the real cause of the conflict. Curious it was, too, how this deeper question ever forced itself to the surface despite effort and disclaimer. No sooner had Northern armies touched Southern soil than this old question, newly guised, sprang from the earth,—What shall be done with Negroes? Peremptory military commands, this way and that, could not answer the query; the Emancipation

Proclamation seemed but to broaden and intensify the difficulties; and the War Amendments made the Negro problems of to-day.

It is the aim of this essay to study the period of history from 1861 to 1872 so far as it relates to the American Negro. In effect, this tale of the dawn of Freedom is an account of that government of men called the Freedmen's Bureau,—one of the most singular and interesting of the attempts made by a great nation to grapple with vast problems of race and social condition.

• • •

The Bureau invited continued cooperation with benevolent societies, and declared: "It will be the object of all commissioners to introduce practicable systems of compensated labor," and to establish schools. Forthwith nine assistant commissioners were appointed. They were to hasten to their fields of work; seek gradually to close relief establishments, and make the destitute self-supporting; act as courts of law where there were no courts, or where Negroes were not recognized in them as free; establish the institution of marriage among ex-slaves, and keep records; see that freedmen were free to choose their employers, and help in making fair contracts for them; and finally, the circular said: "Simple good faith, for which we hope on all hands for those concerned in the passing away of slavery, will especially relieve the assistant commissioners in the discharge of their duties toward the freedmen, as well as promote the general welfare."

No sooner was the work thus started, and the general system and local organization in some measure begun, than two grave difficulties appeared which changed largely the theory and outcome of Bureau work. First, there were the abandoned lands of the South. It had long been the more or less definitely expressed theory of the North that all the chief problems of Emancipation might be settled by establishing the slaves on the forfeited lands of their masters,—a sort of poetic justice, said some. But this poetry done into solemn prose meant either wholesale confiscation of private property in the South, or vast appropriations. Now Congress had not appropriated a cent, and no sooner did the proclamations of general amnesty appear than the eight hundred thousand acres of abandoned lands in the hands of the Freedmen's Bureau melted quickly away. The second difficulty lay in perfecting the local organization of the Bureau throughout the wide field of work. Making a new machine and sending out officials of duly ascertained fitness for a great work of social reform is no child's task; but this task was even harder, for a new central organization had to be fitted on a heterogeneous and confused but already existing system of relief and control of ex-slaves; and the agents available for this work must be sought for in an army still busy with war operations,—men in the very nature of the case ill fitted for delicate social work,—or among the questionable camp followers of an invading host. Thus, after a year's work, vigorously as it was pushed, the problem looked even more difficult to grasp and solve than at the beginning. Nevertheless, three things that year's work did, well worth the doing: it relieved a vast amount of physical suffering; it transported seven thousand fugitives from congested centers back to the farm; and, best of all, it inaugurated the crusade of the New England school marm.

The annals of this Ninth Crusade are yet to be written,—the tale of a mission that seemed to our age far more quixotic than the quest of St. Louis seemed to his. Behind the mists of ruin and rapine waved the calico dresses of women who dared, and after the hoarse mouthings of the field guns rang the rhythm of the alphabet. Rich and poor they were, serious and curious. Bereaved now of a father, now of a brother, now of more than these, they came seeking a life work in planting New England schoolhouses among the white and black of the South. They did their work well. In that first year they taught one hundred thousand souls, and more.

Evidently, Congress must soon legislate again on the hastily organized Bureau, which had so quickly grown into wide significance and vast possibilities. An institution such as that was well-nigh as difficult to end as to begin. Early in 1866 Congress took up the matter, when Senator Trumbull, of Illinois, introduced a bill to extend the Bureau and enlarge its powers. This measure received, at the hands of Congress, far more thorough discussion and attention than its predecessor. The war cloud had thinned enough to allow a clearer conception of the work of Emancipation. The champions of the bill argued that the strengthening of the Freedmen's Bureau was still a military necessity; that it was needed for the proper carrying out of the Thirteenth Amendment, and was a work of sheer justice to the ex-slave, at a trifling cost to the government. The opponents of the measure declared that the war was over, and the necessity for war measures past; that the Bureau, by reason of its extraordinary powers, was clearly unconstitutional in time of peace, and was destined to irritate the South and pauperize the freedmen, at a final cost of possibly hundreds of millions. These two arguments were unanswered, and indeed unanswerable: the one that the extraordinary powers of the Bureau threatened the civil rights of all citizens; and the other that the government must have power to do what manifestly must be done, and that present abandonment of the freedmen meant their practical reenslavement. The bill which finally passed enlarged and made permanent the Freedmen's Bureau. It was promptly vetoed by President Johnson as "unconstitutional," "unnecessary," and "extrajudicial," and failed of passage over the veto. Meantime, however, the breach between Congress

and the President began to broaden, and a modified form of the lost bill
was finally passed over the President's second veto, July 16.

The act of 1866 gave the Freedmen's Bureau its final form,—the form
by which it will be known to posterity and judged of men. It extended
the existence of the Bureau to July, 1868; it authorized additional assistant commissioners, the retention of army officers mustered out of regular service, the sale of certain forfeited lands to freedmen on nominal
terms, the sale of Confederate public property for Negro schools, and a
wider field of judicial interpretation and cognizance. The government of
the unreconstructed South was thus put very largely in the hands of the
Freedmen's Bureau, especially as in many cases the departmental military
commander was now made also assistant commissioner. It was thus that
the Freedmen's Bureau became a full-fledged government of men. It
made laws, executed them and interpreted them; it laid and collected
taxes, defined and punished crime, maintained and used military force,
and dictated such measures as it thought necessary and proper for the
accomplishment of its varied ends. Naturally, all these powers were not
exercised continuously nor to their fullest extent; and yet, as General
Howard said, "scarcely any subject that has to be legislated upon in civil
society failed, at one time or another, to demand the action of this singular Bureau."

To understand and criticise intelligently so vast a work, one must not
forget an instant the drift of things in the later sixties. Lee had surren-
dered, Lincoln was dead, and Johnson and Congress were at loggerheads;
the Thirteenth Amendment was adopted, the Fourteenth pending, and
the Fifteenth declared in force in 1870. Guerrilla raiding, the ever-present
flickering after-flame of war, was spending its forces against the Negroes,
and all the Southern land was awakening as from some wild dream to
poverty and social revolution. In a time of perfect calm, amid willing
neighbors and streaming wealth, the social uplifting of four million slaves
to an assured and self-sustaining place in the body politic and economic
would have been a herculean task; but when to the inherent difficulties
of so delicate and nice a social operation were added the spite and hate
of conflict, the hell of war; when suspicion and cruelty were rife, and
gaunt Hunger wept beside Bereavement,—in such a case, the work of
any instrument of social regeneration was in large part foredoomed to
failure. The very name of the Bureau stood for a thing in the South which
for two centuries and better men had refused even to argue,—that life
amid free Negroes was simply unthinkable, the maddest of experiments.

The agents that the Bureau could command varied all the way from
unselfish philanthropists to narrow-minded busybodies and thieves; and
even though it be true that the average was far better than the worst, it
was the occasional fly that helped spoil the ointment.

Then amid all crouched the freed slave, bewildered between friend and foe. He had emerged from slavery,—not the worst slavery in the world, not a slavery that had made all life unbearable, rather a slavery that had here and there something of kindliness, fidelity, and happiness—but withal slavery, which, so far as human aspiration and desert were concerned, classed the black man and the ox together. And the Negro knew full well that, whatever their deeper convictions may have been, Southern men had fought with desperate energy to perpetuate this slavery under which the black masses, with half-articulate thought, had writhed and shivered. They welcomed freedom with a cry. They shrank from the master who still strove for their chains; they fled to the friends that had freed them, even though those friends stood ready to use them as a club for driving the recalcitrant South back into loyalty. So the cleft between the white and black South grew. Idle to say it never should have been; it was as inevitable as its results were pitiable. Curiously incongruous elements were left arrayed against each other,—the North, the government, the carpet-bagger, and the slave, here; and there, all the South that was white, whether gentleman or vagabond, honest man or rascal, lawless murderer or martyr to duty.

Thus it is doubly difficult to write of this period calmly, so intense was the feeling, so mighty the human passions that swayed and blinded men. Amid it all, two figures ever stand to typify that day to coming ages,— the one, a gray-haired gentleman, whose fathers had quit themselves like men, whose sons lay in nameless graves; who bowed to the evil of slavery because its abolition threatened untold ill to all; who stood at last, in the evening of life, a blighted, ruined form, with hate in his eyes;—and the other, a form hovering dark and mother-like; her awful face black with the mists of centuries, had aforetime quailed at that white master's command, had bent in love over the cradles of his sons and daughters, and closed in death the sunken eyes of his wife,—aye, too, at his behest had laid herself low to his lust, and borne a tawny man-child to the world, only to see her dark boy's limbs scattered to the winds by midnight marauders riding after "damned Niggers." These were the saddest sights of that woeful day; and no man clasped the hands of these two passing figures of the present-past; but, hating, they went to their long home, and, hating, their children's children live to-day.

• • •

The passing of a great human institution before its work is done, like the untimely passing of a single soul, but leaves a legacy of striving for other men. The legacy of the Freedmen's Bureau is the heavy heritage of this generation. To-day, when new and vaster problems are destined to strain every fibre of the national mind and soul, would it not be well to count this legacy honestly and carefully? For this much all men know: despite compromise, war, and struggle, the Negro is not free. In the backwoods of the Gulf States, for miles and miles, he may not leave the plantation of his birth; in well-nigh the whole rural South the black farmers are peons, bound by law and custom to an economic slavery, from which the only escape is death or the penitentiary. In the most cultured sections and cities of the South the Negroes are a segregated servile caste, with restricted rights and privileges. Before the courts, both in law and custom, they stand on a different and peculiar basis. Taxation without representation is the rule of their political life. And the result of all this is, and in nature must have been, lawlessness and crime. That is the large legacy of the Freedmen's Bureau, the work it did not do because it could not.

I have seen a land right merry with the sun, where children sing, and rolling hills lie like passioned women wantoned with harvest. And there in the King's Highway sat and sits a figure veiled and bowed, by which the traveler's footsteps hasten as they go. On the tainted air broods fear. Three centuries' thought has been the raising and unveiling of that bowed human heart, and now behold a century new for the duty and the deed. The problem of the Twentieth Century is the problem of the color-line.

Chicago: A. C. McClurg and Co.

MISSISSIPPI IN THE 1930s AND 1940s

Clyde Cox, the highly regarded head of the English Department at Jacksonville State University from 1972 to 1996, grew up in Corinth, Mississippi, during the 1930s and 1940s, not long after Wright left for Chicago in 1927. His perspective interacts with Wright's in provocative ways, making it clear, for instance, why the two men, had they met and been the same age, could never have talked frankly with each other, even with the best of intentions on both their parts. One of the goals of the system was to preclude honest communication between blacks and whites: racism cannot withstand analysis. The author interviewed Cox in Jacksonville, Alabama.

INTERVIEW WITH CLYDE COX (1996)

Felgar: According to the narrator in *Black Boy*, the white South said it knew "niggers," but it did not know him. Do you agree with this statement? Why or why not?

Cox: I agree completely with the narrator. Even with open communication, objectivity, and empathy, it is difficult to know anyone—let alone a race. Most of the people who made the statement (and one heard it daily) thought because they could predict the reactions of blacks in situations where whites determined every given, they knew blacks. A German trooper with a machine gun knew Jews in Dachau to the same extent. And I think that one of the factors that probably simply cannot be imagined adequately is the absoluteness to the segregation and the severity with which blacks were "kept in their place."

Felgar: Wright plays three roles in *Black Boy*: author, narrator, character. In each role the reader can detect anxiety about whether Wright thought he would be trusted. How did you, as a white, male Mississippian, deal with the issue of trust in the different roles black Mississippians had to take around you?

Cox: Looking back, I realize that, although I was around blacks when I was growing up, I only came to know, reasonably well, two. One, a WW II vet, was comrade and confidant in a work place (drugstore) where he, at twenty-eight and father of two children, was the janitor and delivery boy. Our duties overlapped to the extent that I was janitor/delivery boy when I was so needed, but also a clerk (a position he was not allowed to hold). We bonded, at least partially, because we worked for a tyrant we both despised. I trusted him altogether—learned from him about the black world, which he *seemed* to discuss openly after we had become well acquainted, and about the war, which, in the forties, was *the* fascinating subject for those of us who had missed it. Perhaps it is relevant to mention, in regard to trust, that I was invited to his home twice and went; he never visited my home though he was invited on several occasions.

The other black was valet, bootlegger, pimp (whatever he had to be to keep the job) at the best hotel in Corinth. He had been a childhood friend of Father and took me aside on several occasions, when I was in high school, to lecture me on my conduct. He talked directly to me (no "sirs," etc.), shamed me, even, on one occasion, tongue-lashed me. He always took me aside for these talks. He was, by the way, always wise in his counseling, and I very much respected him.

Felgar: Wright almost always makes judgments about the black women in the book based on their physical appearance. Do you recall this attitude toward black women as being true of both black and white males when you were growing up?

Cox: I grew up among working class people and moved, except for school functions, among that class, almost exclusively. In all male settings, there always seemed to be someone (older adolescents or adults, usually) who assessed all women in physical terms, unless an authority figure, pious or dictatorial or both, was present. Matriarchs of both colors were usually spared description, but all young females came in for it.

Felgar: In the unexpurgated version of *Black Boy*, Wright is asked a pornographic question about his anatomy. What would you say the question may reveal about white male attitudes toward the sexuality of black males?

Cox: I don't know the particular question you mention, but our notions, as white boys, were boringly stock: blacks had sex at every opportunity; were much better equipped sexually; were completely uninhibited. I suppose that our notions suggest our feelings of inadequacy about performance generally. . . .

Felgar: At one point in *Black Boy*, some white men encourage Wright and another young black man called Harrison to box each other for the amusement of the whites. Did you observe similar incidents when you were growing up in Mississippi?

Cox: No. As a youngster of five or so I witnessed a razor fight between two young black men. My grandfather tried to talk them into stopping, shaming them about such a fray in the presence of children, and warning them about the dangers of razors. They ignored him and went at it. I did hear of such amusements but cannot honestly say that I knew of anyone who had ever witnessed one.

Felgar: Wright had very little use for the black church and yet many have argued that, at least until recently, it was the center of the black community. Would you agree that Wright underestimated its value, at least based on what you observed in the 1930s and 40s?

Cox: From what little I saw, the black church was enormously important. It was perhaps the only place where even white lawmen were hesitant to parade and bully. (It was *not* a sanctuary.) Certainly black preachers, in my opinion, were the most respected figures in the black community, by blacks and whites generally. (I'm uneasy here: I was in four black churches in my life. In two instances, to play music; in the other two, to hear it.)

Felgar: Blacks outnumbered whites in Mississippi when you and Wright were growing up there, and yet Wright makes it very clear that the black community was absolutely terrified of angry whites. How would you account for this?

Cox: Corinth was only seven percent black. But to ignorant people, the world is only a few blocks, or miles at most, wide. Too, there were no black cops, no access to real weapons. The local national guard company, complete with machine guns, was all white.

Felgar: Wright seems to view black life in the South from 1908 to 1927 (the year he was born and the year he went to Chicago) as hopeless. Considering that many talented and resourceful blacks stayed in the South, and considering what you saw a little later, would you say Wright exaggerated the bleakness of African American life then?

Cox: The situation must have seemed hopeless to a bright, highly sensitive young black man, particularly one who was intellectual by nature. . . . I do remember blacks were, quietly, making progress financially even in the grim conditions they faced.

Felgar: How did blacks manage to survive in Mississippi if, as Wright suggests, their situation was so bleak?

Cox: Here Faulkner's rhetoric is not hyperbolic: the resilience of the human spirit. Not only did people survive, white and black, but often with a great deal of humor expressed while surviving—or maybe the sense of humor is what helped?

Felgar: How much, and what kind of, social life did you observe between blacks and whites in Mississippi?

Cox: Virtually none.

Felgar: Wright is extremely worried in *Black Boy* that the reader not think he spoke and wrote black English as an adult. Do you recall a similar anxiety among some black people in the 1930s and 40s? What would you attribute this worry to?

Cox: I knew no educated blacks. The blacks I came in contact with were not concerned with the subtleties of language at all. There were, of course, the Mr. [Malaprops] in the black community—always the source of delight to whites as evidence of white superiority: "Did you hear 'Reverend' McAmos come in down at the hardware store complaining that the temperature was below zero?" Thigh slapping all around.

Felgar: Wright is also deeply apprehensive that the reader not think he ended up a "black peasant," like his father. How much classism do you recall in the black and white communities?

Cox: Class considerations were everywhere, based on a variety of things: "aristocratic" ancestors; Christian sect (an Episcopalian was simply upper-class); property; cultural sophistication (real or imagined); club membership. From the insults blacks directed at other blacks, it seemed to me that all of the above were common with them, too. They often added distinctions of blackness: "You so black yo' own Mammy cain't fin' you after sundown." (I offer this example because I actually heard it more than once.)

STUDY QUESTIONS

1. Do you see any indications today that the thinking that informs the Black Code of Mississippi, Jim Crow laws, and the 1890 Constitution is still alive?

2. View the film *The Birth of a Nation*, which depicts Reconstruction from an extremely racist perspective. Do you think it should be banned? Why or why not?

3. After viewing *The Birth of a Nation* and *Gone with the Wind*, to what extent are their perspectives on Reconstruction shared by the whites in *Black Boy*?

4. Why could Booker T. Washington and W.E.B. Du Bois not afford the purity of Wright's point of view in *Black Boy*? Are they worried about more than Wright is in his autobiography?

5. Is Washington just a sellout, or is he hoping blacks can get at least one foot on America's social and economic ladder?

6. Would Wright have made a good politician?

7. Why is Wright so much less willing to compromise than Washington is?

8. Why would someone like Washington, who was willing to conceal his deepest feelings, be so offensive to Wright?

9. How does the chapter from *The Souls of Black Folk* help you understand the bitterness of Wright's maternal grandfather?

10. Of the three writers—Washington, Du Bois, and Wright—who could be accurately categorized as black folk? Why?

11. Which writer has the most distinctive voice? Justify your opinion.

12. Would you say that Wright might have benefited from a broader, less personal perspective, such as that of Du Bois in chapter 2 of *The Souls of Black Folk*; or, since *Black Boy* is a fictionalized autobiography and not history, is Wright justified in being so much more personal and subjective than Du Bois is?

13. In historical terms, how much difference might it have made if whites like Clyde Cox had been given the opportunity to develop honest relationships with African Americans in the 1930s and 1940s?

14. What functions were served by keeping the two races alienated from each other?

15. Why would wealthy southern whites be especially interested in encouraging the estrangement of blacks and working-class whites?

16. Today, it is fairly common in the South to see blacks and whites

working together, but still unusual to see them in each other's homes. How would you account for this?

TOPICS FOR WRITTEN OR ORAL EXPLORATION

1. Divide the class into three groups, one representing Wright's point of view on the deferred dream of black equality, another Du Bois', and the third Washington's. Debate the issue of whose point of view is most likely to bring about black equality.

2. The Reconstruction Period in American history is still debated; write a research paper investigating the question of how valid the views of it in this chapter are.

3. How much of your own sense of who you are is race-based? Is race a legitimate source of authority? Again, what would Wright, Du Bois, and Washington say?

4. Some white Americans have spent a tremendous amount of time, energy, and money trying to deny the undeniable humanity of African Americans. Can a person prove that she or he is human, or does this have to be taken on faith? What would you do if you had to prove you were human? Is that what Wright is really trying to do in *Black Boy*? Does/can he succeed?

5. Write a paper comparing and contrasting the writing styles of Washington, Du Bois, and Wright. How would you account for their differences?

SUGGESTED READINGS

Brock, William Ranulf. *An American Crisis: Congress and Reconstruction, 1865–1867*. New York: St. Martin's Press, 1963.

Clemenceau, Georges. *American Reconstruction*. New York: Da Capo Press, 1969.

Crowe, Charles Robert, ed. *The Age of Civil War and Reconstruction, 1830–1900*. Homewood, Ill.: Dorsey Press, 1966.

Foner, Eric. *America's Reconstruction*. New York: Harper Perennial, 1995.

Kennedy, Stetson. *After Appomattox: How the South Won the War*. Gainesville: University Press of Florida, 1995.

Lindsey, David. *Americans in Conflict: The Civil War and Reconstruction*. Boston: Houghton Mifflin, 1973.

McKitrick, Eric L. *Andrew Johnson and Reconstruction*. New York: Oxford University Press, 1988.

Nash, Howard Pervear. *Andrew Johnson: Congress and Reconstruction*. Rutherford, N.J.: Fairleigh Dickinson University Press, 1972.
Reid, Whitelaw. *After the War*. Cincinnati: Moore, Wilstach, and Baldwin, 1866.
Richter, William L. *The ABC-CLIO Companion to American Reconstruction*, 1862–1877. Santa Barbara, Calif.: ABC-CLIO, 1996.
Thomas, Emory M. *The American War and Peace, 1860–1877*. Englewood Cliffs, N.J.: Prentice-Hall, 1973.

5

Race and Racism,
Then and Now

Although race has been one of the most powerful influences in shaping American society, as *Black Boy* makes all too clear, it is almost completely incoherent as an idea. It is not unusual, for instance, for there to be more genetic differences between people within a racial category than there are between people in different racial categories: a "black" person, then, might have more genes in common with a "white" person than with some other "black" person, but in society's eyes this scientific fact would make no difference. Or consider the infamous one-drop rule that declares that one drop of "black" blood makes a person "black." Of course everyone's blood is red, and one could easily ask why one drop of "white" blood does not make a person "white." When slavery was legal, many plantation owners were happy with the rule because it enabled them to count every child with black ancestors as a slave, but after the abolition of slavery, the rule worked to the advantage of the African American community by increasing the size of the population perceived as black. Wright's maternal grandmother could easily have passed as white, but she chose to remain in the black community and was thus considered black.

Consider also the reactions to Oprah Winfrey's wearing contact lenses that made her eyes green, or Michael Jackson's frequent visits to the hospital for plastic surgery. That some people feel so strongly about what a black person (or any other person) "should" look like is very telling. One might well ask why a person should not look any way she or he pleases, or, indeed, why there is such an obsession with physical appearance in America. There is no mention in the Declaration of Independence of what an American should look like, but everyone knows anyway: an American should be male and white. Wright chose the "wrong" race.

One is led to wonder why a concept so easily exposed as dubious has been taken so seriously by so many people for so long. Who stands to lose if the idea of race is jettisoned? The answer can only be those who profit from racial identity as an unearned source of authority, which in many cases means white men. Presumably, if the white males in *Black Boy* were certain that they were superior to blacks, they would welcome competition or be indifferent to it because they would automatically prevail. And yet Reynolds and Pease, who, Wright claims, drove him off his job at the first optical company, fear Wright as a potential economic competitor.

Today, such treatment of blacks would be recognized as racism, but the situation is more complicated. For example, Spike Lee, the African American film director, has argued that it is impossible for a black American to be a racist; when challenged, Lee said he meant that blacks could not engage in institutional racism, because they do not control the institutions of this country. Or consider the Clarence Thomas–Anita Hill controversy. Thomas told the white male senators at his confirmation hearing that he was a victim of an electronic lynching, knowing that they would think of the lynching of black men; he did not remind them that black women were lynched, too, so Thomas's charge of racism may have been complicated by the senators' ignorance. The most controversial example of racism recently, though, involved the O. J. Simpson criminal trial, in particular Simpson attorney Robert Shapiro's charge that Simpson's other lead attorney, Johnny Cochran, "played the race card." Shapiro meant that Cochran convinced the jury that Simpson was or may have been a victim of white racism, particularly in the collection of evidence. But Simpson's possible guilt and white racism are not necessarily related. That is, Simpson may well have committed two murders whether or not there was a racist police conspiracy against him. Shapiro was suggesting that because whites and blacks have had such different experiences in the American criminal justice system, Cochran was hoping that by exploiting that fact, he would get Simpson acquitted.

The constant in the history of racism is that it is the judgment of people based on stereotypical categories rather than on the basis of individual traits. Thus, someone might believe that whites or Asians are smart, that blacks are athletic, or that black men are lustier than nonblack men. In other words, racism is discrimination or prejudice or categorization based on racial stereotypes rather than on empirical evaluation of individuals, regardless of racial status. But it may be the case that members of racially oppressed minorities cannot afford the luxury of judging whites empirically.

The documents in this chapter show attitudes about race and racism throughout the twentieth century. The excerpt from Joseph Alexander Tillinghast's book, *The Negro in Africa and America*, would be hilarious if the consequences of such ludicrous notions had not been so deplorable. Ray Stannard Baker, in a study of lynching published three years before Wright was born, tends to see it as a social problem that society will have to be patient about; he focuses almost exclusively on the point of view of the lynchers rather than that of the victims. William Graham Sumner views race and racism as rather quaint but harmless notions, whereas the French anthropologist Jean Finot sees racism as morally wrong but not because blacks are not inferior to whites. Alfred Holt Stone's article presents a mixed view of the racial situation in the first decade of the twentieth century. The most notorious opinions included here are expressed by Senator Theodore Bilbo, who used racism to further his political career. Two contemporary essays reflect current challenges to racism. Jonathan Tilove expounds on mutual distrust between blacks and whites as an ongoing legacy of slavery. William C. Singleton III contends that the notion of racial categories is going to have to expand to accommodate the increasing complexity of "race."

AFRICANS AS CHILDREN

The first document in this chapter would be extremely amusing if the prejudices expressed therein were not still widely, if less openly, held. Joseph Alexander Tillinghast, an American anthropologist, saw in West Africa, where Wright's African ancestors probably came from, what he believed: that Africans are hopelessly inferior to whites but may still benefit from contact with them. He used a nonexistent culture, a fantasy based on pseudoscience and ignorance, to bolster his own racial vanity: Could he help it, he seems to ask his readers, if he and his culture were superior to all other nonwhite people and cultures? It is this woeful provincialism and arrogance that Wright is up against in *Black Boy*. The whites think it goes without saying that they are "better" than blacks, but they almost never realize that the idea of superiority is incoherent and insupportable. What makes Tillinghast's views so disturbing is that he does not recognize that they make no sense or that they could be challenged by counter-evidence. Wright and his fellow African Americans are in the preposterous position in *Black Boy* of having to act as though they believe they are inferior to people who clearly are not superior. But being truthful, that is, resisting the kind of thinking expressed by Tillinghast, could be dangerous to blacks, and thus the whites mistake their silence as an indication of agreement. Everyone pretends to agree with the argument of someone who is pointing a gun at them.

FROM JOSEPH ALEXANDER TILLINGHAST, *THE NEGRO IN AFRICA AND AMERICA* (1902)

Preface

The present study does not claim to be an addition to human knowledge. One familiar with the writings of travelers and ethnologists on the negroes in West Africa is acquainted with most of the books out of which the first few chapters have been woven; one acquainted with the history and present condition of the race in the United States, has met most of the statements and arguments embodied in the later portions of the work. The merit of the book, in my judgment, is to be found rather in

the fact that it brings together two lines of investigation which have hitherto been kept asunder. The rapidity with which an uncivilized people
may be lifted, or may lift themselves, to the plane of the advanced civilization is still undetermined. To realize that many characteristics of the
American Negro are part of his inheritance from Africa, and were bred
into the race there long generations, may perhaps strengthen the patience and forbearance of those who seek to expedite his progress. To
realize that many faults often attributed to the debasing effects of American slavery, are faults which he shares with his African ancestors and
contemporaries, may suggest a juster and more impartial view of the
merits and demerits of the economic system which crumbled as a result
of the Civil War. That a southern white man, the son of a slave holder,
should have selected this subject for investigation, have pursued his work
at a northern university, utilizing for the purpose a library, the nucleus
of which in this field is a large anti-slavery collection, and have reached
results, the tendency of which seems to me eirenic rather than controversial, is a noteworthy sign of the times, suggesting how both sections
and both races are coming more and more to cooperation of effort and
harmony of conclusions regarding our great problem. The work of Mr.
Tillinghast has given me much light upon a question in which for years
I have been interested, and I believe that many others of his readers will
share my judgment.

Walter Willcox
Ithaca, New York

Our knowledge of certain of the relations between the mind and its physiological basis in the brain may be taken as fairly established. Although
some have set much store on comparison of brain weights, it is felt by
conservative anthropologists that the difficulties of using this criterion
are too great for it to be of much value. Cranial capacity, however, offers
one not so open to objection. It has been found that in this respect the
Australian aborigines stand lowest, Africans next, Mongolians next, and
highest of all, Caucasians. Reference to tables given by Topinard, shows
that while the cranial capacity of the European ranges from 1,550 cubic
centimeters upward in the male, and 1,350 in the female, that of the West
African ranges from 1,430 and 1,257 respectively. Taylor quotes figures
from Professor Flower, giving a mean cranial capacity of 79 cubic inches
for the Australian, 85 for the African, and 91 for the Caucasian. Nowhere
is it questioned that the Negro possesses less cranial capacity than the
Mongolian or the Caucasian.

But more significant than this, perhaps, is the qualitative comparison
of structure and texture in the brain. Topinard says that in the African
the secondary convolutions are less complex and rich in minute structure

than in the European. Professor A. H. Keane cites with approval the dictum of Waitz: "That the convolutions in the negro brain are less numerous and more massive than in the European appears certain." Keane himself reaches the conclusion that mental energy and capacity depend most intimately upon "the sinuosities or convolutions of the inner white substance, and especially upon the cellular tissue of the thin outer cortex or envelope of grey matter, which follows all the inner convolutions, with which it is also connected by an exceedingly complex nervous system." It is in the structured differences that the greatest significance no doubt lies.

One other factor greatly affecting ultimate mental development, is the length of the period of immaturity, during which the mind remains plastic. Keane says: "The development of cellular tissue, with a corresponding increase of mental power, apparently goes on till arrested by the closure of the cranial sutures. All the serratures are stated to be more complex in the higher than in the lower races, and their definite closing appears to be delayed until a later period in life amongst the former than amongst the latter. This physiological character . . . has recently been noticed by two intelligent observers, Col. Ellis among the Upper Guinea peoples, and Capt. Binger among the west Sudanese generally. "The black is a child," says this writer, "and will remain so"; and the sudden arrest of the mental faculties at the age of puberty is attributed to the closing of the sutures. "There seems much probability, too, in the opinion of some, that the marked development of sexual activity among West Africans, with the arrival of puberty, absorbs energy at the expense of mental force." Ellis, whose opinion is referred to above, writes as follows: "In early life they evince a degree of intelligence, which, compared with that of the European child, appears precocious; and they acquire knowledge with facility until they arrive at the age of puberty, when the physical nature masters the intellect, and frequently completely deadens it. This peculiarity . . . has been attributed by some physiologists to the early closing of the sutures of the cranium, and it is worthy of note that throughout West Africa it is by no means rare to find skulls without any apparent transverse or longitudinal sutures." The fact that African children learn easily until the age of puberty, but fail to progress after that time, may be due to another consideration apparently overlooked by the above writers, viz., the difference in the character of knowledge to be acquired in earlier and later stages of education. In the earlier stages it is chiefly the perceptive and imitative facilities, together with memory that are required, but little of the higher faculties of abstract reasoning. These conditions become gradually reversed, however, as the student advances into highly elaborated realms of knowledge. That the African begins to halt on reaching this later stage of acquisition, may be owing to the want of a quality of mind not to be found in brains of coarser texture.

• • •

In whatever respect, therefore, we consider the physiological basis of mental power, whether as to size of brain, or its inner structure, or the length of its plastic period, the natives of Guinea are at a grave disadvantage in comparison with the Caucasian. The low stage of their culture can hardly be deemed the accidental effect of external conditions, for it has its counterpart in the inner constitution of the role. This is what we should expect, knowing that selection operating through many generations brings about a close physical and psychical adaption of the organism to its environment. We have seen what the West African environment is, and it is obvious that no great industrial system, no science, and no art could be self-developed there in the first instance; but it is also plain that without the rise of these secondary agencies of selection, the psychic nature could never be adapted to grasp such attainments. The consideration of the general laws of biologic evolution would thus lead us, aside from the evidence above adduced, to believe that the mind of a lower tropical race is unfitted to assimilate the advanced civilization of a strenuous and able northern race.

Yet it could be hasty to conclude that the West Africans are incapable of progress. Though below the modern Caucasian in capacity to master vast knowledge, to handle intricate machinery, and to carry on self-government, they may be able to profit from judicious education and to respond to new stimuli to exertion. With the advent of new standards of efficiency, selection would operate to bring forward those best fitted to the new regime, provided that competition of abler peoples did not enter upon the scene so soon as to overthrow and crush all alike. As for obvious reasons this seems unlikely to happen in West Africa, its inhabitants may have a creditable future before them. Where portions of the race have been removed into other regions, and placed in the midst of able and strenuous competition, the case is altogether different.

The temperamental qualities of the race present some marked and interesting peculiarities. In common with all peoples of low culture, the West Africans are unstable of purpose, dominated by impulse, unable to realize the future and restrain present desire, callously indifferent to suffering in others, and easily aroused to ferocity by the sight of blood or under great fear. More peculiar to themselves are a pronounced aversion to silence and solitude, a passionate love of rhythm in sound and motion, an excessive excitability, and utter lack of reserve.

Nothing so well reveals high development or is so vital to the welfare of a great society as the power to bridle passion, steady the emotions, and keep fixedly to a definite purpose. Infirmity of will means weakness at the rest of life. Now, the West Africans give evidence of a marked deficiency in will power throughout every phase of their existence. Their intense emotions, strong sexual passion, their cupidity, their erratic impulses, are continually breaking control, even at the cost of immediate disaster. The white man from the north, foreseeing, sure-footed, and iron-willed, at first witnesses the infatuated rashness with exasperated amazement, but in the end with resigned patience.

Illustrations of this weakness are strewn thickly through all works on West Africa. A pen-picture of store-keeping in that region is given by Miss Kingsley: "Whether the native is passing in a bundle of rubber or a tooth of ivory or merely cashing a *bon* (a local check on the store) for a week's bush catering, he is, in Congo Français [the French Congo], incapable of deciding what he will have, when it comes to the point. He comes into the shop with a bon in his hand, and we will say, for example, the idea in his head that he wants fish-hooks—'jupeo' he calls them—but, confronted with the visible temptation of pomatum, he hesitates, and scratches his head violently. Surrounding him there are ten or twenty other natives with their minds in a similar wavering state, but yet anxious to be served forthwith. In consequence of the stimulating scratch, he remembers that one of his wives said he was to bring some lucifer matches, another wanted cloth for herself, and another knew of some rubber she could buy very cheap, in tobacco, of a Fan woman, who had stolen it. This rubber he knows he can take to the trader's store and sell for pocket handkerchiefs of a superior pattern, or gunpowder, or rum, which he cannot get at the mission store. He finally gets something and takes it home, and likely enough brings it back in a day or so, somewhat damaged, desirous of changing it for some other article or articles. Remember, also, that these Bantu, like the negroes, think externally in a loud voice; also, like Mr. Kipling's 'oout,' 'he smells most awful vile,' and . . . accompanies his observations with violent dramatic gestures; and let the customer's tribe or sex be what it may be, the customer is sadly, sadly liable to pick up any portable object within reach, under the shadow of his companions' uproar, and stow it away in his armpits, between his legs, or, if his cloth be large enough, in that.

The difficulties encountered by Du Chaillu every time he started from an African village with his train of porters are thus described. "When all was arranged—when everybody had taken leave of all his friends, and come back half a dozen times to take leave once again, or say something before forgotten—when all the shouting, and ordering, and quarreling were done, and I had completely lost patience, we at last got away." Here we have the violently excitable, demonstrative negro, garrulous to the last degree and absolutely heedless of time. Whenever a number of them are together, and they are never seen otherwise, they raise "a perfect word-fog," as Miss Kingsley calls it. Every emotion finds instant and un-reserved expression. In joy, in grief, in anger, it is always the same—infinite and unfeared volubility. Tylor notes the perplexing fact that, with no great differences in climatic or physical environment the Indian of Brazil is dull and stoical, while the negro of West Africa overflows constantly with "eagerness and gaiety."

This impulse to a lively, noisy sociability, molds the racial habits in many ways. Regardless of temperature, there must invariably be blazing fires at night in each village, around which the crowd may gather and make merry. Bright moonlight is always the signal for all-night carousals, accompanied by infinite noise in the shape of tom-tom beating, gun-firing, native music and dancing, etc.

It is but another phase of inconstancy that the West African is never long weighed down by sorrow or misfortune. His cheerfulness seems irrepressible. He is incapable of nursing long the feelings of anger or revenge, let the provocation be what it may. Barbot remarks that the natives seem "very little concerned at misfortune, so it is hard to perceive any change in them," and he goes on to say, "when they have gained victory over their enemies, they return home dancing and singing, and if they have been beaten and totally routed, still they dance, feast, and make merry. The most they do in the greatest adversity is to shave their heads and make some alteration in their garments: but they still are ready to feast about graves, and should they see their country in a flame, it would not disturb their dancing, singing and drinking; so that it may well be said, according to some authors, that they are insensible to grief or want." At the first news of death or disaster there is an outburst of demonstrative grief, but in an amazingly brief time none could tell that anything gloomy had happened. In the moment of discovering a great wrong or injury, there is an outburst of fierce anger, which in a few hours or days, at most, subsides into the habitual easy-going mood.

They are passionately fond of music, and it exerts a very great influence upon their lives. They have several kinds of rude musical instruments. Easily first among them all is the tom-tom, a drum made of a hollow section of a log with a skin stretched tightly over one end. The tom-tom accompanies the army to the field, the corpse to its grave, the bridegroom to his wedding, the royal embassy on its journey. Not a festival of any kind can proceed without it. Beaten in rhythmical fashion, and with an art that to the native expresses definite ideas, its power over him seems irresistible. Dr. Chaillu says: "It is curious what a stirring effect the sound of the tom-tom has on the African. It works upon him like martial music does upon excitable Frenchmen; they lose all control over themselves at its sound, and the louder and more energetically the horrid drum is beaten the wilder are the jumps of the male African, and the more disgustingly indecent the contortions of the women." They have other instruments, horns made of elephant tusks, hollowed out and with holes flute fashion, so that various notes can be blown; also complex instruments, consisting of calabashes of different sizes, with orifices tightly covered with stretched skins; and a few other devices of similar characters for producing musical notes.

Music is used, says Ellis, "with three objects, i.e., to stimulate the religious sentiment, the military spirit, and the sexual passion. In the first case the priests have early seen its influence, and have applied it to their own purposes; chiefs and rulers utilize it in the second case, and the youth of the towns and villages in the third, when the drums sound for moonlight dances." Their numerous dances are invariably accompanied with music and singing. The religious dances, performed by the priests and their special devotees, are wild rhythmic leanings and movements of the body, accompanied by facial contortions, expressive, in the eyes of the people, of possession by a spirit. The popular dances chiefly appeal to the sexual nature. Barbot thus describes them: "The men and women who are to compose the dance divide themselves into equal numbers and couples, opposite to each other, and forming a general dance, they meet and fall back again, leaping, beating their feet hard on the ground, bowing their heads to each other, and snapping their fingers, muttering some words at times, and speaking loud; then whispering in each other's ears, moving now very slowly and then very fast; men and women running against each other, breast to breast . . . clapping their hands together, throwing their elephant's tail at one another or clapping it about their shoulders." Somewhat refined of its grosser features, this dance survives on American soil as the modern negro "cake-walk." In West Africa, however, these dances exhibit all degrees of sexual suggestion, and to civilized whites they appear indescribably indecent. Dr. Chaillu found himself irresistibly moved to depart from the scene of more than one dance especially given in his honor, although he ran serious risk of offending his hosts. No description of the dances could be ventured in his books. These facts are further evidence of the great power in this tropical race of sexual instinct which dominates even the most public festivals.

The racial existence of the Guinea native for ages in the jungles of torrid Africa has given time for the processes of adaptation to do their full work undisturbed. Physical or mental energy have never been exacted or favored by the conditions, nor a genius for searching out labor-saving devices; foresight and self-mastery have not been vital amid prodigal nature and loosely organized society; and so, the Negro in his original habitat has been bred to a happy-go-lucky, improvident existence. For him life is to be taken light-heartedly, never minding the disaster of yesterday or forecasting to-morrow's trouble. He is attracted irresistibly to music and uproarious gaiety, and the more sex suggestion in it the better. When anger or fear arises, the tiger in him is out in a flash and somebody dies a bloody death. At all times and under all circumstances, he carries his emotions on his face and tongue, passionately loves companionship, and forgets each day's sorrow with the sunset.

New York: Macmillan, pp. 92–101.

LYNCHING

This selection clarifies what Wright faced when he refers to lynching in *Black Boy*: whites who engaged in it not only did not see the depravity of their actions, they felt moral indignation toward those who tried to prevent lynchings or to convict those responsible for the crime. The exhilaration and carnival-like atmosphere of lynchings, as Baker's article makes clear, made them irresistible to the lynchers and terrifying to the black community. They served the function of keeping black people "in their place," but not as effectively as the white mobs and their supporters hoped. Rape was often the crime with which the lynching victim was charged, even though it was extremely rare for a black man to rape a white woman.

In *Black Boy* Wright is more interested in the psychological and emotional effects of lynching than in the physical horror of it. (He does convey that horror in a poem, "Between the World and Me," and in a photograph in *12 Million Black Voices*.) In his autobiography he makes it clear that lynching was always an unspoken threat, and thus constantly operated as a terror tactic to intimidate the black community. If a black male could be hanged just for looking at a white woman, then it is no wonder that Wright is both fascinated and frightened when the naked prostitute walks in front of him in the hotel where he works (Ralph Ellison, the author of *Invisible Man*, claims that this actually happened to him). The racial situation was so bad when Wright was growing up that black organizations were not able to get federal legislation passed that might have helped put an end to the lynching of black people. For Wright, lynching was one more example of the irrational violence that he saw almost everywhere as he grew up.

The author of the following excerpt, Ray Stannard Baker (1870–1946), was the official biographer of President Woodrow Wilson. He also wrote *Following the Color Line* (1908) and *Native American* (1941), edited *McClure's Magazine* and the *American Magazine*, and served as a special commissioner for the State Department. By the racial standards of early twentieth-century America, Baker's attitude toward lynching would have been considered enlightened. But he never considers how he would react if he or someone he cared for deeply were the intended victim of a lynching; that is precisely one of Wright's points in *Black Boy*—one "understands" lynching only if she or he is its object. Baker is also not immune to the stereotype that black men are particularly prone to savagery.

FROM RAY STANNARD BAKER, "WHAT IS A LYNCHING? A STUDY OF MOB JUSTICE, SOUTH AND NORTH" (1905)

Statesboro, Georgia, where two negroes were recently burned alive under the most shocking circumstance, is a thrifty county-seat of some two thousand five hundred people, located about seventy miles from Savannah. For a hundred years a settlement has existed here, but it was not until the people discovered the wealth of the turpentine forests and of the sea-island cotton industry that the town became highly prosperous. Since 1890, it has doubled in population every five years. Most of the town is newly built. A fine, new court-house stands in the city square, and there are new churches, a large, new academy, a new water-works system and telephones, electric lights, rural free delivery—everywhere the signs of improvement and progress. It is distinctly a town of the New South, developed almost exclusively by the energy of Southerners and with Southern money. Its population is pure American, mostly of old Carolina, Georgia, and Virginia stock. Fully seventy per cent of the inhabitants are church members—Baptists, Presbyterians, and Methodists—and the town has not had a saloon in twenty-five years and rarely has a case of drunkenness. There are no beggars and practically no tramps. A poorhouse, built several years ago, had to be sold because no one would go to it. The farms are small, for the most part, and owned by the farmers themselves; only eight per cent of them are mortgaged. Schools are plentiful for both white and colored children, though the school year is short and education not compulsory.

In short, this is a healthy, temperate, progressive American town—a country city, self-respecting, ambitious, with a good future before it—the splendid future of the New South.

About forty per cent of the population of the county consists of negroes. To most Northerners a negro is a negro; but one of the first things to impress a visitor in the South is the fact that there are two very distinct kinds of negroes—as distinct as the classes of white men. The first of these is the self-respecting, resident negro. Sometimes he is a land-owner, more often a renter; he is known to the white people, employed by them, and trusted by them. The Southerner of the better class, indeed, takes a real interest in the welfare of the home negro, and often has a real affection for him. In Statesboro, as in most of the South, a large proportion of the negroes are of this better class. On the other hand, one finds everywhere large numbers of the so-called "worthless negroes," perhaps a growing class, who float from town to town, doing rough work, having no permanent place of abode, not known to the white population generally. The turpentine industry has brought many such negroes to the neighborhood of Statesboro. Living in the forest near the turpentine-stills, and usually ignorant and lazy, they and all their kind, both in the country districts and in the city, are doubly unfortunate in coming into contact chiefly with the poorer class of white people, whom they often meet as industrial competitors. White bricklayers, for instance, work with negro bricklayers, and the trade jealousy which inevitably arises is slowly crowding the negro out of the skilled trades and forcing him, more and more, to the heavy toil of manual labor. This industrial friction (a more important factor in the negro problem, perhaps, than is commonly recognized), added to the historic contempt of the negro for the "poor white" and the hatred of the poor white for the negro, constitutes a fertile source of discord. Even after making due allowance for the bitter problems of "social equality," negro franchise, and negro crime, all of which go to make up what is called "race prejudice," it is safe to say that if there were only the better class of whites in the South and the better class of negroes, there would be no such thing as a negro problem.

• • •

About six miles from the city of Statesboro lived Henry Hodges, a well-to-do planter. He had a good farm, he ran three plows, as they say in the cotton country, and rumor reported that he had money laid by. Coming of an old family, he was widely related in Bulloch County, and his friendliness and kindness had given him and his family a large circle of acquaintances. Family ties and friendships, in old-settled communities like those in the South, are influences of much greater importance in fixing public opinion and deciding political and social questions than they are in the new and heterogenous communities of the North.

• • •

On the evening of July 29, 1904, Mr. Hodges drove to a neighbor's house to bring his nine-year-old girl home from school. No Southern white farmer, especially in thinly settled regions like Bulloch County, dares permit any woman or girl of his family to go out anywhere alone, for fear of the criminal negro. "You don't know and you can't know," a Georgian said to me, "what it means down here to live in constant fear lest your wife or daughter be attacked on the road, or even in her home. Many women in the city of Statesboro dare not go into their back yards after dark. Every white planter knows that there is always danger for his daughter to visit even the nearest neighbor, or for his wife to go to church without a man to protect her."

It is absolutely necessary to understand this point of view before one can form a true judgment upon conditions in the South.

When Hodges arrived at his home that night, it was already dark. The little girl ran to join her mother; the father drove to the barn. Two negroes—perhaps more—met him there and beat his brains out with a stone and a buggy brace. Hearing the noise, Mrs. Hodges ran out with a lamp and set it on the gate-post. The negroes crept up—as nearly as can be gathered from the contradictory stories and confessions—and murdered her there in her doorway with peculiar brutality. Nearly all of the crimes committed by negroes are marked with almost animal-like ferocity. Once aroused to murderous rage, the negro does not stop with mere killing; he bruises and batters his victim out of all semblance to humanity. For the moment, under stress of passion, he seems to revert wholly to savagery.

The negroes went into the house and ransacked it for money. The little girl, who must have been terror-stricken beyond belief, hid behind a trunk; the two younger children, one a child of two years, the other a mere baby, lay on the bed. Finding no money, the negroes returned to their homes. Here they evidently began to dread the consequences of their deed, for towards midnight they returned to the Hodges home. During all this time the little girl had been hiding there in the darkness, with the bodies of her father and mother in the doorway. When the negroes appeared, she either came out voluntarily, hoping that friends had arrived, or she was dragged out.

"Where's the money?" demanded the negroes.

The child got out all she had, a precious five-cent piece, and offered it to them on condition that they would not hurt her. One of them seized her and beat her to death.

I make no excuse for telling these details; they *must be told*, else we shall not see the depths or the lengths of this problem.

The negroes then dragged the bodies of Mr. and Mrs. Hodges into their home and set the house afire. As nearly as can be made out from the subsequent confessions, the two younger children were burned alive. When the neighbors reached the scene of the crime, the house was wholly consumed, only the great end chimney left standing, and the lamp still burning on the gate-post.

Well, these Southerners are warm-hearted, home-loving people. Everyone knew and respected the Hodges—their friends in the church, their many relatives in the county—and the effect of this frightful crime described in all its details, may possibly be imagined by Northern people living quietly and peacefully in their homes. When two of the prominent citizens of the town told me, weeks afterwards, of the death of the little girl, they could not keep back the tears.

The murder took place on Friday night; on Saturday the negroes, Paul Reed and Will Cato, were arrested with several other suspects, including two negro preachers. Both Reed and Cato were of the illiterate class; both had been turpentine workers, living in the forest, far from contact with white people. Cato was a floater from South Carolina. Reed was born in the county, but he was a good type of the worthless and densely ignorant negro.

It is a somewhat common impression that a whole town loses itself in a passion of anarchy, and is not satisfied until the criminals are killed. But in spite of the terrible provocation and the intense feeling, there yet existed in Statesboro exactly such a feeling for the sacredness of law, such intelligent Americanism, as exists in your town or mine. Not within the present generation had a lynching taken place in the town, and the people were deeply concerned to preserve the honor and good name of their community. In the midst of intense excitement a meeting of good citizens, both white and black, was called in the court-house. It was presided over by J. A. Brannan, one of the foremost citizens. Speeches were made by Mayor Johnstone, by the ministers of the town, and by other citizens, including a negro, all calling for good order and the calm and proper enforcement of the law.

And the regular machinery of justice was put in motion with commendable rapidity. Fearing a lynching, the negroes were sent to Savannah and there lodged in jail. A grand jury was immediately called, indictments were found, and in two weeks—the shortest possible time under the law—the negroes were brought back from Savannah for trial. To protect them, two military companies, one from Statesboro, one from Savannah, were called out. The proof of guilt was absolutely conclusive, and, although the negroes were given every advantage to which they were entitled under the law, several prominent attorneys having been appointed to defend them, they were promptly convicted and sentenced to be hanged.

In the meantime great excitement prevailed. The town was crowded for days with farmers who came flocking in from every direction. The crime was discussed and magnified; it was common talk that the "niggers of Madison County are getting too bigoty"—that they wouldn't "keep their place." Fuel was added to the flame by the common report that the murderers of the Hodges family were members of a negro assassination society known as the "Before Day Club," and wild stories were told of other murders that had been planned, the names of intended victims even being reported.

On the Sunday night before the trial, two negro women, walking down the street, pushed two respectable white girls off the sidewalk, with obscene abuse. The crowd dragged the women from a church where they had gone, took them to the outskirts of the town, whipped them both violently, and ordered them to leave the county.

"Let the law take its course," urged the good citizen. "The negroes have been sentenced to be hanged, let them be hanged legally; we want no disgrace to fall on the town."

But as the trial progressed and the crowd increased, there were louder and louder expressions of the belief that hanging was too good for such a crime. I heard intelligent citizens argue that a tough negro criminal, in order to be a hero in the eyes of his people, does not mind being hanged. He is allowed to make a speech, the ministers pray over him, he confesses dramatically, and he and all his negro friends are sure that he is going straight to Paradise.

Another distinct feeling developed—a feeling that I found in other lynching towns: that somehow the courts and the law were not to be trusted to punish the criminals properly. Although Reed and Cato were sentenced to be hanged, the crowd argued that "the lawyers would get them off," that "the case would be appealed, and they would go free." Members of the mob tried to get Sheriff Kendrick to promise not to remove the negroes to Savannah, fearing that in some way they would be taken beyond the reach of justice.

In other words, there existed a deep-seated conviction that justice too often miscarried in Bulloch County and that murderers commonly escaped punishment through the delays and technicalities of the law.

• • •

I am not telling these things with any idea of excusing or palliating the crime of lynching, but with the earnest intent of setting forth all the facts, so that we may understand just what the feelings and impulses of a lynching town really are, good as well as bad. Unless we diagnose the case accurately, we cannot hope to prescribe effective remedies.

In the intense, excited crowd gathered around the court-house on this Tuesday, the 16th of August, other influences were also at work, influences operating in a greater or lesser degree in every lynching mob. We are accustomed to look upon a mob as an entity, the expression of a single concrete feeling; it is not; it is itself torn with dissensions and compunctions, swayed by conflicting emotions. Similarly, we look upon a militia company as a sort of machine, which, set in operation, automatically performs a certain definite service. But it is not. It is made up of young men, each with his own intense feelings, prejudices, ideals; and it requires unusual discipline to inculcate such a sense of duty that the individual soldier will rise superior to the emotions of the hour. Most of these young men of Statesboro and Savannah really sympathized with the mob; among the crowd the Statesboro men saw their relatives and friends. Some of the officers were ambitious men, hoping to stand for political office. What would happen if they ordered the troops to fire on their neighbors?

And "the nigger deserved hanging," and "why should good white blood be shed for nigger brutes?" At a moment of this sort the clear perception of solemn abstract principles and great civic duties fades away in tumultuous excitement. Yet these soldier boys were not cowards; they have a fighting history; their fathers made good soldiers; they themselves would serve bravely against a foreign enemy, but when called upon for mob service they have failed repeatedly, both North and South.

Up to the last moment, although the crowd believed in lynching and wanted to lynch, there seemed to be no real and general determination to forestall the law. The mob had no center, no fixed purpose, no real plan of action. One determined man, knowing his duty (as I shall show in another story), and doing it with common sense, could have prevented trouble, but there was no such man. Captain Hitch, of the Savannah Company, a vacillating commander, allowed the crowd to pack the courthouse, to stream in and out among his soldiers; he laid the responsibility (afterwards) on the sheriff, and the sheriff shouldered it back upon him. In nearly all the cases I investigated, I found the same attempt to shift responsibility, the same lack of a responsible head. Our system too often fails when mob stress is laid upon it—unless it happens that some splendid man stands out, assumes responsibility, and becomes a momentary despot.

A mob, no matter how deeply inflamed, is always cowardly. This mob was no exception. It crowded up, crowded up, testing authority. It joked with the soldiers, and when it found that the jokes were appreciated, it took further liberties; it jostled the soldiers—good-humoredly. "You don't dare fire," it said, and the soldiers made no reply. "Your guns aren't loaded," it said, and some soldier confessed that they were not. In tender consideration for the feelings of the mob, the officers had ordered the men not to load their rifles. The next step was easy enough; the mob playfully wrenched away a few of the guns, those behind pushed forward, knowing they will not be hurt—and in a moment the whole mob was swarming up the stairs, yelling and cheering.

In the court-room sentence had been passed on Reed and Cato, and the judge had just congratulated the people on "their splendid regard for the law under very trying conditions." Then the mob broke in. A brother of the murdered Hodges, a minister from Texas, rose splendidly to the occasion. With tears streaming down his face, he begged the mob to let the law take its course.

"We don't want religion, we want blood," yelled a voice.

The mob was now thoroughly stirred; it ceased to hesitate; it was controlled wholly by its emotions. The leaders plunged down the court-room and into the witness chamber, where the negroes sat with their wives, Reed's wife with a young baby. The officers of the law accommodatingly indicated the right negroes, and the mob dragged them out. Hanging was at first proposed, and a man even climbed a telegraph-pole just outside the court-house, but the mob, growing more ferocious as it gathered volume and excitement, yelled its determination:

"Burn them! burn them!"

They rushed up the road, intending to take the negroes to the scene of the crime. But it was midday in August, with a broiling hot sun overhead and a dusty road underfoot. A mile from town the mob swerved into a turpentine forest, pausing first to let the negroes kneel and confess. Calmer spirits again counseled hanging, but some one began to recite in a high-keyed voice the awful details of the crime, dwelling especially on the death of the little girl. It worked the mob into a frenzy of ferocity.

"They burned the Hodges and gave them no choice; burn the niggers!"

"Please don't burn me," pleaded Cato. And again: "Hang me or shoot me; please don't burn me!"

Some one referred the question to the father-in-law of Hodges. He said Hodges' mother wished the men burned. That settled it. Men were sent into town for kerosene oil and chains, and finally the negroes were bound to an old stump, fagots were heaped around them, and each was drenched with oil. Then the crowd stood back accommodatingly, while a photographer, standing there in the bright sunshine, took pictures of the chained negroes. Citizens crowded up behind the stump and got their faces into the photograph. When the fagots were lighted, the crowd yelled wildly. Cato, the less stolid of the two negroes, partly of white blood, screamed with agony; but Reed, a black, stolid savage, bore it like a block of wood. They threw knots and sticks at the writhing creatures, but always left room for the photographer to take more pictures.

And when it was all over, they began, in common with all mobs, to fight for souvenirs. They scrambled for the chains before they were cold, and the precious links were divided among the populace. Pieces of the stump were hacked off, and finally one young man—it must be told—gathered up a few charred remnants of bone, carried them up-town, and actually tried to give them to the judge who presided at the trial of the negroes, to the utter disgust of that official.

American Magazine, January 1905.

THE PLANTATION TRADITION

Early in the twentieth century the sociologist William Graham Sumner looked back to the pre–Civil War South as a time when blacks and whites lived happily together. His view is distorted by the plantation tradition, the notion that before the Civil War slaves were happy and contented children who had no complaints and just wanted to be left alone to pick cotton and sing and dance. The war ruined this idyllic way of life, so the tradition goes. Sumner obviously had not spoken to Wright's maternal grandfather, who fought for the Union and gladly killed Confederate soldiers. One of Wright's targets in *Black Boy* is the ludicrous notion that blacks, during or after slavery, were happy with the racial situation. No white person, Wright suggests, would have been content for a second in the subservient position assigned to blacks.

William Graham Sumner should be clearly distinguished from the better-known Charles Sumner, the abolitionist senator from Massachusetts who was badly beaten by Congressman Brooks from South Carolina in 1856 because Sumner had insulted the reputation of South Carolina.

FROM WILLIAM GRAHAM SUMNER, *FOLKWAYS: A STUDY OF THE IMPORTANCE OF USAGES, MANNERS, CUSTOMS, MORES, AND MORALS* (1906)

Blacks and whites in southern society. In our southern states, before the civil war, whites and blacks had formed habits of action and feeling towards each other. They lived in peace and concord, and each one grew up in the ways which were traditional and customary. The civil war abolished legal rights and left the two races to learn how to live together under other relations than before. The whites have never been converted from the old mores. Those who still survive look back with regret and affection to the old social usages and customary sentiments and feelings. The two races have not yet made new mores. Vain attempts have been made to control the new order by legislation. The only result is the proof that legislation cannot make mores. We see also that mores do not form under social convulsion and discord. It is only just now that the new society seems to be taking shape. There is a trend in the mores now as they begin to form under the new state of things. It is not at all what the humanitarians hoped and expected. The two races are separating more than ever before. The strongest point in the new code seems to be that any white man is boycotted and despised if he "associates with negroes." Some are anxious to interfere and try to control. They take their stand on ethical views of what is going on. It is evidently impossible for any one to interfere. We are like spectators at a great natural convulsion. The results will be such as the facts and forces call for. We cannot foresee them. They do not depend on ethical views any more than the volcanic eruption on Martinique contained an ethical element. All the faiths, hopes, energies, and sacrifices of both whites and blacks are components in the new construction of folkways by which the two races will learn how to live together. As we go along with the constructive process it is very plain that what once was, or what any one thinks ought to be, but slightly affects what, at any moment, is. The mores which once were are a memory. Those which any one thinks ought to be are a dream. The only thing with which we can deal are those which are.

New York: Ginn and Co., pp. 77–78.

NOBLE SAVAGES

Race Prejudice was published by the French sociologist Jean Finot in 1906, two years before Wright was born. Far more level-headed than Tillinghast, Finot nevertheless sees blacks as children of nature, naive creatures who will become more responsible when whites treat them better. Wright confronts his readers with the obvious in *Black Boy*: blacks are no more childlike than anybody else, although some whites persist in seeing them that way. But Wright does agree with Finot on one key point: the race problem is a white problem, not a black problem, because the whites have the power and thus make the racial rules. If whites want the racial problem to be solved, they will have to change their attitude toward blacks. That is one of Wright's goals in *Black Boy*: to tell his white readers that blacks react the same way whites would if the situation were reversed, with bitter humor, anger, resentment, and fear. How else would a human being react to being treated as something other than human? So, for example, Wright is understandably outraged when, in chapter 6 of *Black Boy*, a white woman interviewing him for a job asks whether he steals. Unfortunately, Finot might well have asked Wright the same question.

FROM JEAN FINOT, *RACE PREJUDICE* (1906)

But when the slaves of the prejudice of races see themselves forced to render justice to the Negro intelligence which is equal in every way to that of the Whites, they console themselves, at the risk of being taxed with partiality, with the thought of the "innate" immorality of the blacks.

Herein we find a regrettable inferiority, so say the detractors of Negroes, and with them all the anthropologists who believe in the "fatality" of blood and of colour. This accusation must fall before facts. In vain do the enemies of the Negro race endeavor to convince us that their bad qualities increase with education. Statistics, to which belongs the decisive voice, are a standing refutation of their assertion. Moreover, where Negro criminality is very great, it deserves a special absolution.

The coloured population is still going through one of its most critical periods. In one day it found itself thrown from slavery into freedom, without any moral or material resources. It was necessary to cut a path through life at the cost of superhuman efforts. Far from being encouraged by its old masters in the way of moral perfection, it has never ceased to be the butt of their railleries and persecutions. The North, in its desire to humiliate the South, did the greatest harm to these children of nature in according to them there and then the fullest political rights. Called to vote, the Negroes, with all their limitations and illiteracy, did their best to envenom still further their relations with the Whites. Vain like children and intoxicated with the power which came so suddenly into their hands, they lost all sense of reality. Work being to them synonymous with slavery, they considered all occupation to be incompatible with liberty. Idle and vain, they played with life like dogs do with objects which fall between their paws. In their heedlessness and want of comprehension of the world which they entered without the least preparation, they very soon lost all balance, together with that little Christian morality which had been taught them in servitude. Those who had had the benefit of a liberal education were soon discouraged by the disdain of the Whites and the difficulty of earning their bread.

The number of coloured *declassé* was growing, as all could see, and with it the number of criminals. Little by little their eyes were opened. Men of goodwill and initiative from among the Whites of the North, like General Armstrong, and from among Negroes, like Booker Washington, saw that in the present state of things the future belonged to professional teaching, and they directed their efforts on this side. Thus a second revolution took place in the inner life of Negroes which made them better men and more dignified. Even apart from these extenuating circumstances, the Negroes need not lower their heads before the Whites. It would be fastidious to compare in detail the number of white criminals with that of coloured people. Let us note, however, that the increase of coloured inhabitants in a locality does not increase the rate of criminality. The proportion remains the same. The Negroes are especially accused of being at variance with the Code in the North. In this, Negro writers like Booker Washington and Professor [D]u Bois, &c., tell us there is nothing astonishing. The Negroes come there especially from the South, living on the outskirts of society sometimes for reasons known to the police of the localities from which they come, and sometimes as immigrants looking for work.

But when they have reached the North, they find themselves subject to the persecutions of the syndicates of work. Discouraged and famished, they often succumb to the temptations of despair and misery.

But in the North as well as in the South the number of convictions in no way corresponds with the criminality of Negroes. The jury composed of Whites is frankly hostile to them. Not only do the police harass them and bring them before tribunals for the least thing, but these tribunals also condemn them for the smallest offences. In certain Southern States there is even a kind of special premium which gives an impetus to the conviction of Negroes. For their keep in the prisons brings in considerable profits to the States, to say nothing of the middleman. A Negro prisoner as such is obliged to work on farms and in mines and industries. It is calculated that a prisoner generally brings in about 750 francs to the State. In most cases White contractors, worse than the old planters, harshly exploit their work and enrich themselves at their expense. Everyone, from the State to the contractor, is thus interested in heavy penalties. For the longer the imprisonment, the more the revenues of the State and of the exploiter of Negro labour increase.

Owing to the prejudices and the hatred of the judges, the Negroes have to put up with convictions which are often unjust, and which are nearly always more severe than those meted out to Whites. Frequently, when a disorder breaks out in a Negro center, a disorder the causes of which are often mysterious, a kind of raffle takes place among them. Arrested, accused, and condemned to pay large fines, the poor Blacks find it impossible to pay. A White benefactor then appears, and, after having reimbursed the sums fixed by the tribunal, takes the Negroes into his service in virtue of a public contract.

These shocking abuses of judicial power ought rather to increase the sum of White criminality, which is thus weighted with the charge of partiality and injustice! They are made, however, to increase that of the Blacks.

After all, can one decently ask from a race exasperated by all kinds of barbarous and unjust treatment, that self-respect and moral dignity which constitute the best barriers against criminal leanings?

Let us add that certain of their crimes are only of a transitory character. Such are the small thefts which are so objected to in Negroes. During the period of slavery the Blacks were deprived of all property. Everything which they succeeded in acquiring belonged by right to their masters. The Negro, not being able to take possession of the property of another, did not really steal. He displaced but in no way diminished his master's wealth. The latter in any case remained the proprietor of everything which belonged to his slaves. Booker Washington tells the funny story of a slave who after stealing his master's chickens justified himself in this way: "Now, Massa, it is true you have a little less chicken; but, Massa, you have a little more Negro." Conceptions rooted in the Negro conscience for centuries cannot disappear in a summer's night. Let us content ourselves with saying that really educated Negroes are unharmed by them. This is an evident proof that theft is not in the Negro blood. It is only the temporary result of a special mentality, of a particular state of soul, of which the Whites are in the first place the most guilty.

The same applies to their family life. One reproaches them with immorality, forgetting that marriage and the family only date among coloured folk from the emancipation. In the time of slavery there were neither husbands, wives, parents, nor children. The master disposed of the life and well-being of his slaves as of his other chattels. Mulattoes, who number more than two millions, are there to bear testimony to the respect of the planters for the chastity of Negro women in general and for their own conjugal life in particular! The women were separated from their husbands as it pleased their masters, the children were transported if necessary far from their parents, the young girls were delivered to the caprice of the planters and their employees, and all this with the aid of the law, which admitted no resistance on the part of those interested; such is the account of family life in the old days. How could it flourish in a *milieu* from which one never ceased to banish it?

The liberty accorded to men of colour was powerless to revive in a day virtues which perhaps never existed. One must allow time to work. Seconded by the moral and intellectual culture which Negroes of to-day enjoy, they will be allowed to rise to the level of the Whites. . . .

Whenever the vitality and the future of the White races are dealt with, there is much concern as to the birth-rate amongst them. With reason or without, there is seen in the numerical increase of the population a symptom of health and a criterion as to the part which history has in store for it. From this point of view, the coloured folk of the States are far ahead of the Russians and the Italians, who are regarded as the most prolific of peoples. Whereas other Americans, by themselves and not including immigrants, are diminishing in number, the coloured population never ceases to grow.

Since 1860 (we must leave out the period before the liberation of the Negroes, which was marked by an incessant arrival of slaves from Africa) the Negro population has more than doubled. From about five millions in 1870 it became six millions and a half in 1880, seven millions and a half in 1890, and about nine millions in 1900.

At the present time about 280 American counties, with an extent of about 150,000 square miles, contain a Negro population numbering far more than that of the Whites, there being about 130 Blacks to every 100 Whites.

A serious crime against chastity weighs heavily on the Negro conscience, viz. the rape of White women. This fact saddens profoundly the best among the Negroes, as also those Whites who really sympathize with them. Without wishing to find excuses for Negro criminality on this matter, we must observe that its gravity is apt to be measured by the indignation of the Whites rather than by the true number of crimes committed. Lynching singularly changes the nature of justice in very often making people suspected of a crime first the accused and then the victims. The Negroes reply, however, with reason that the crime of rape is not unknown among the Whites, who indeed practice it on a large scale.

Immoral men are equally to be despised, whatever may be the colour of their skin. White men who commit this crime against Negro women are equal to the Negroes who are guilty of it against White women. Let us not forget, however, that all the cases of lynching are not solely due to outrages against White women. According to certain American statistics, there were lynched in the Southern States, from 1891 to 1902, 1,862 persons, of whom only 1,448 were for attacks against women, 770 for murders, &c.

This kind of justice, however, or rather injustice, has the effect of giving rise to the very crimes which it is intended to stifle. Exasperated by the stupid ferocity of crowds, Negroes avenge themselves in multiplying the crimes which seem to touch their persecutors the most. American legislators understand this so well that they are now waging a war to the death against lynching in general and against that caused by the rape of White women in particular.

The profound transformations which are being effected in the lives of the Blacks will alone cause this crime to cease. Both coloured agriculturists and educated Negroes are exempt from it. Its complete disappearance only depends on the Whites themselves. Let them try to be more just towards the Negroes, let them strive to make amends towards them for the crimes of the past, let them be penetrated with the idea that the virtue of a coloured woman is equal to that of a White, let them beware of lynching in particular (that incomparable breeding ground for the multiplication of evil instincts), and this crime which desolates the Whites of the South will gradually die away. It will entirely disappear when the two races shall have understood that they only form two arms of the same body, and that on their friendship and fraternal work depends the happiness of the Southern States.

New York: E. P. Dutton, pp. 229–308. Translated by Florence Wade-Evans.

RACIAL FRICTION

The American sociologist Alfred Holt Stone, writing in 1907, describes the complexity of the racial situation at the time. On the one hand, he thinks that it goes without saying that whites are "better" than blacks, but on the other hand, some blacks are understandably unwilling to accept white domination. Stone has no doubt that most blacks, those who do not carry the genes of the "master" race, are content and docile, but he never imagined Richard Wright and *Black Boy*.

FROM ALFRED HOLT STONE, "IS RACE FRICTION BETWEEN
BLACKS AND WHITES IN THE UNITED STATES GROWING AND
INEVITABLE?" (1907–1908)

Thus we return to the first branch of our inquiry—the attitude of the negro as one of the determining factors in the increase or decrease of race friction. It is more difficult to answer for him than for the white man. The latter has a history in the matter of his relations with other races, perfectly well defined to anyone who will study it candidly. He has either ruled or ruined, to express it in a few words, and pretty often he has done both. It has been frequently said that the negro is the only one of the inferior, or weaker, or backward, or undeveloped races (the terms are largely interchangeable and not at all important), which has ever looked the white man in the face and lived. But for all the significance the statement holds, we have only to go to Aesop's fable of the tree which would, and the tree which would not bend before the storm. I know of no race in all history which possesses in equal degree the marvelous power of adaptability to conditions which the negro has exhibited through many centuries and in many places. His undeveloped mental state has made it possible for him to accept conditions, and to increase and be content under them, which a more highly organized and sensitive race would have thrown off, or destroyed itself in the effort to do so. This ability to accept the status of slavery and to win the affection and regard of the master race, and gradually but steadily to bring about an amelioration of the conditions of the slave status made possible the anomalous and really not yet understood race relations of the *antebellum* South. The plain English of the situation was that the negro did not chafe or fret and harass himself to death, where the Indian would have done so, or massacred the white man as an alternative. In many respects the negro is a model prisoner—the best in this country. He accepts the situation, generally speaking; bears no malice; cherishes no ill will or resentment, and is cheerful under conditions to which the white man refuses to reconcile himself.

This adaptability of the negro has an immediate bearing on the question before us. It explains why the negro masses in the southern states are content with their situation, or at least not disturbing themselves sufficiently over it to attempt to upset the existing order. In the main, the millions in the South live at peace with their white neighbors. The masses, just one generation out of slavery and thousands of them still largely controlled by its influences, accept the superiority of the white race, as a race, whatever may be their private opinion of some of its members. And, furthermore, they accept this relation of superior and inferior, as a mere matter of course—as part of their lives—as something neither to be questioned, wondered at, or worried over. Despite apparent impressions to the contrary, the average southern white man gives no more thought to the matter than does the negro. As I tried to make clear at the outset, the status of superior and inferior is simply an inherited part of his instinctive mental equipment—a concept which he does not have to reason out. The respective attitudes are complementary, and under the mutual acceptance and understanding there still exist unnumbered thousands of instances of kindly and affectionate relations—relations of which the outside world knows nothing and understands nothing. In a Boston colored magazine some months since, Miss Augusta P. Eaton gives an account of her settlement work among negroes in that city. In describing relations where colored and white families live in contact, she says, "The great bond of fellowship is never fully established. There is tolerance, but I have found few cases of friendly intimacy." Here is just the difference between the two situations. "Friendly intimacies," probably not in the sense meant by Miss Eaton, but friendly and kindly intimacies, none the less, do exist in the South, despite all we hear to the contrary. They are the leaven of hope and comfort for white and black alike in what does appear to be a pretty big lump of discord. In the mass, the southern negro has not bothered himself about the ballot for more than twenty years, not since his so-called political leaders let him alone; he is not disturbed over the matter of separate schools and cars, and he neither knows nor cares anything about "social equality."

I believe there may develop in process of time and evolution a group of contented people, occupying a position somewhat analogous to that of the Jamaican peasant class, satisfied in the enjoyment of life, liberty, and the pursuit of happiness, and afforded the full protection of the law. I believe it is possible for each of the various groups of the two races which find themselves in natural juxtaposition to arrive at some basis of common occupancy of their respective territories which shall be mutually satisfactory, even if not wholly free from friction. I express a belief that this is possible, but to its accomplishment there is one absolute condition precedent; they must be let alone and they must be given time. It must be realized and accepted, whether we like it or not, that there is no cut-and-dried solution of such problems, and that they cannot be solved by resolutions or laws. The process must be gradual and it must be normal, which means that the final basis of adjustment must be worked out by the immediate parties in interest. It may be one thing in one place and another thing in another place, just as the problem itself differs with differences of local conditions and environment. We must realize that San Francisco is not Boston, that New Orleans is not New York. Thus much for the possibilities as to rank and file.

But what of the other class? The "masses" is at best an unsatisfactory and indefinite term. It is very far from embracing even the southern negro, and we need not forget that seven years ago there were 900,000 members of the race living outside of the South. What of the class, mainly urban and large in number, who have lost the typical habit and attitude of the negro of the mass, and who, more and more, are becoming restless, and chafing under existing conditions? There is an intimate and very natural relation between the social and intellectual advance of the so-called negro and the matter of friction along social lines. It is in fact only as we touch the higher groups that we can appreciate the potential results of contact upon a different plane from that common to the masses in the South. There is a large and steadily increasing group of men, more or less related to the negro by blood and wholly identified with him by American social usage, who refuse to accept quietly the white man's attitude toward the race. I appreciate the mistake of laying too great stress upon the utterances of any one man or group of men, but the mistake in this case lies the other way. The American white man knows little or nothing about the thought and opinion of the colored men and women who today largely mold and direct negro public opinion in this country. Even the white man who considers himself a student of "the race question" rarely exhibits anything more than profound ignorance of the negro's side of the problem. He does not know what the other man is thinking and saying on the subject. This composite type which we poetically call "black," but which in reality is every shade from black to white, is slowly developing a consciousness of its own racial solidarity. It is finding its own distinctive voice, and throughout its own books and papers and magazines, and through its own social organizations, is at once giving utterance to its discontent and making known its demands.

And with this dawning consciousness of race there is likewise coming

an appreciation of the limitations and restrictions which hem in its un-
folding and development. One of the best indices to the possibilities of
increased racial friction is the negro's own recognition of the universality
of the white man's racial antipathy toward him. This is the one clear note
above the storm of protest against the things that are, that in his highest
aspiration everywhere the white man's "prejudice" blocks the colored
man's path. And the white man may with possible profit pause long
enough to ask the deeper significance of the negro's finding of himself.
May it not be only part of a general awakening of the darker races of the
earth? Captain H. A. Wilson, of the English army, says that through all
Africa there has penetrated in some way a vague confused report that far
off somewhere, in the unknown, outside world, a great war has been
fought between a white and a yellow race, and won by the yellow man.
And even before the Japanese-Russian conflict, "Ethiopianism" and the
cry of "Africa for the Africans" had begun to disturb the English in South
Africa. It is said time and again that the dissatisfaction and unrest in India
are accentuated by the results of this same war. There can be no doubt
in the mind of any man who carefully reads American negro journals that
their rejoicing over the Japanese victory sounded a very different note
from that of the white American. It was far from being a mere expression
of sympathy with a people fighting for national existence against a power
which had made itself odious to the civilized world by its treatment of
its subjects. It was, instead, a quite clear cry of exultation over the defeat
of a white race by a dark one. The white man is no wiser than the ostrich
if he refuses to see the truth that in the possibilities of race friction the
negro's increasing consciousness of race is to play a part scarcely less
important than the white man's racial antipathies, prejudices, or whatever
we may elect to call them.

In its final analysis the sum and substance of the ultimate demand of
those Americans of African descent whose mental attainments and social
equipment identify them much more closely with the Anglo-Saxon than
with the negro masses, is definitely and clearly stated in the words of Dr.
[Du Bois]:

There is left the last alternative—the raising of the negro in America
to full rights and citizenship. And I mean by this, no half-way measures; I mean full and fair equality. That is, the chance to obtain
work, regardless of color, to aspire to position and preferment on
the basis of desert alone, to have the right to use public conve-
niences, to enter public places of amusement on the same terms as
other people, and to be received socially by such persons as might
wish to receive them. These are not extravagant demands, and yet
their granting means the abolition of the color line. The question
is, Can American negroes hope to attain to this result?

With equal clearness and precision, and with full comprehension of its larger meaning and significance and ultimate possibilities, the American white man answers the question in the language of another eminent American sociologist. Professor Edward A. Ross, in contrasting the attitudes of Anglo-Saxons and Latins toward other races on this continent, says:

> The superiority of a race cannot be preserved without pride of blood and an uncompromising attitude toward the lower races. . . . Whatever may be thought of the [latter] policy, the net result is that North America from the Behring Sea to the Rio Grande is dedicated to the highest type of civilization; while for centuries the rest of our hemisphere will drag the ball and chain of hybridism.

And thus the issue is joined. And thus also perhaps we find an answer to our own question, whether racial friction in this country is increasing and inevitable.

American Journal of Sociology 13 (1907–1908): 676–697.

CENSORSHIP

One of the worst of the race-baiting politicians in Mississippi, sometimes known as Prince of the Peckerwoods, was Senator Theodore Bilbo, who read the following statement into the *Congressional Record* in 1945. His remarks are directed to his white supporters in Mississippi, who know they can depend on him to maintain the racist status quo. The tactics used by politicians like Bilbo and George Wallace, the former governor of Alabama, are particularly pernicious; if the racial situation were reversed, that is, if racist blacks had had the upper hand over whites, and Bilbo and Wallace had been black, both politicians would have been happy to engage in racist tirades against whites. Their only real concern was attracting votes: they did not care whether one race was really "better" than another, and in Wallace's case, he knew better anyway. Note Bilbo's contradictory position: No one should be allowed to read *Black Boy*, but if his colleagues read it, they will see why it is so popular.

FROM THEODORE BILBO, REMARKS ABOUT *BLACK BOY* MADE
BEFORE THE U.S. SENATE (1945)

There is another book which should be taken off the book racks of the Nation; it should be removed from the bookstores; its sale should be stopped. It is the recent book of the month, which has had such a great sale. Senators can understand why it has had such a sale if they will read it. It is entitled "Black Boy," by Richard Wright. Richard Wright is a Mississippean. He was born and reared near Natchez, Miss. He went from Natchez to Jackson, from Jackson to Memphis, from Memphis to Chicago, and from Chicago to Brooklyn, N.Y., where he is married to a white woman and is living happily, he says. He wrote the book Black Boy ostensibly as the story of his life. Actually it is a damnable lie from beginning to end. It is practically all fiction. There is just enough truth to it to enable him to build his fabulous lies about his experiences in the South and his description of the people of the South and the culture, education, and life of Southern people. The purpose of the book is to plant the seeds of hate in every Negro in America against the white men of the South or against the white race anywhere, for that matter. That is the purpose. Its purpose is to plant the seeds of devilment and troublebreeding in the days to come in the mind and heart of every American Negro. Read the book if you do not believe what I am telling you. It is the dirtiest, filthiest, lousiest, most obscene piece of writing that I have ever seen in print. I would hate to have a son or daughter of mine permitted to read it; it is so filthy and so dirty. But it comes from a Negro, and you cannot expect any better from a person of his type.

Congressional Record, 79th Congress, 1st Session, 128 (June 27, 1945): 91.

SLAVERY'S LEGACY OF DISTRUST

The following article, by Jonathan Tilove, helps to explain why Wright and other black Americans cannot afford to trust whites, which then leads to the question of whether whites can afford to trust blacks. American slavery and its consequences have not been faced honestly yet and may never be, considering how painful the experience is likely to be.

The narrator in *Black Boy* says that "if [he] ever really hotly hated unthinking whites, it was" when they muddied the steps he had just cleaned at a research hospital in Chicago; "never had I felt so much the slave as when I scoured those stone steps each afternoon." It may be very difficult, if not impossible, for white readers of *Black Boy* to think that this incident was the only time Wright "hotly hated" whites (note, too, the qualification "unthinking"), but he may be trying to convince such readers that he almost always judges whites as individuals rather than as members of a category. If he lets his white readers know that he has deep and understandable doubts about them in the light, among other things, of what some of their ancestors did to his ancestors, they may well resist the idea of reading Wright's autobiography. One of the effects of slavery, then, is to complicate Wright's relationship to his readers.

FROM JONATHAN TILOVE, "SCARS OF SLAVERY" (1994)

On the slave ships carrying Africans to America, the whites and blacks each viewed the other as cannibals.

To the whites the supposed savageness of black Africans was used to justify their enslavement. To the blacks, what the whites were doing to them suggested they were fully capable of the ultimate evil.

And so, from their very first contact on their way to America, blacks and whites have had utterly different perceptions of reality where race is a factor.

Whether it's a white person crossing the street to avoid encountering a young black male (stereotyped as the modern savage), or a black person telling a pollster that O. J. Simpson is being framed, or that crack or AIDS

[is] a conspiracy against the black community (whites' endless capacity for evil), the alternate realities born in slavery persist.

"The individual unifying cultural memory of black people," writes Columbia University law professor Patricia Williams, who is black, "is the helplessness of living under slavery or in its shadow."

Where whites sometimes see what appears to them to be black paranoia and a black obsession with race, blacks see what appears to them to be white denial, an unwillingness or inability to connect the dots to reveal the true contours of racism.

To blacks, slavery, and then Jim Crow, are the prima facie evidence of the extraordinary lengths whites will go to oppress and degrade them. If they could do that, the thinking runs, what wouldn't they do, even if today it is done more subtly.

As the old joke goes, any black in America who isn't paranoid is crazy.

If slavery and its aftermath do not inform a person's vision of race, says psychiatrist William Grier, that vision is distorted.

"If you don't go back to slavery, you'd have to assume that all living blacks are geniuses at digging a hole for themselves," says Grier, the co-author of the 1968 classic, *Black Rage*.

But, he says, that's what whites commonly do.

"There is an inclination on the part of white people to deny the history of race in this country, to say that race relations began when they were born, that they haven't lynched anybody, they haven't enslaved anybody, so that all that stuff's irrelevant," says Grier, who is black and lives in San Diego.

Political scientist Paul Sniderman, co-author of *The Scar of Race*, which examines racial attitudes, warns there is a danger in indulging this sense of historical grievance.

First, he thinks that angry victimology is much more common among those blacks who end up being quoted in the newspaper than in the black community at large. When he listens to black focus groups, says Sniderman, who is white, he hears little sympathy for those who seek to blame others for their problems.

Furthermore, he says that absorption with grievance blinds those blacks who subscribe to it to what his polling indicated are improving, and more flexible, white racial attitudes.

Mohammed Naseehu Ali, a black African from Ghana who has been in the United States for several years, attending first boarding school and now Bennington College in Vermont, also sees a self-destructive edge in many black Americans' obsession with a history of mistreatment.

"They take the burden of their history, what happened to the slaves, what happened to their grandfathers or their fathers, and they nurse it in their hearts," says Ali.

While he, for example, saw the O. J. Simpson case simply as a tragedy, he noticed a tendency on the part of black Americans to embrace Simpson as a victim "even if he's completely wrong."

"White people look at it more for what it is," says Ali. But then he adds, tellingly, "maybe that's because they think they don't have anything to lose."

When race is involved, though, blacks seldom feel they have nothing to lose.

Patricia Turner, a professor of African-American and African studies at the University of California, Davis, recalls as a child her parents' relief when they learned that the man who killed all those student nurses in Chicago, Richard Speck, was white. It was the same relief they felt whenever someone notorious in the news was not black, says Turner.

Turner, author of *I Heard It Through the Grapevine: Rumor in African-American Culture*, suspects that even some blacks who believe Simpson is probably guilty do not want to tell a white pollster that.

And, says Patricia Williams, the New York law professor, there is good reason for such feelings of racial identity.

Williams, in her book, *The Alchemy of Race and Rights*, recalls the case of Tawana Brawley, the black teenager who said she was kidnapped, raped and abused by a group of white men in upstate New York. When her story fell apart, Williams says, the cry went up: "Who will ever again believe a black woman who cries rape by a white man?"

And yet, Williams says, when it turned out that Charles Stuart, a white Bostonian, lied when he accused a black man of murdering his pregnant wife to hide his own guilt, "There was not a story I could find that carried on about 'who will ever believe' the next white man who cries murder."

If blacks exercise a double standard on race, it is, some argue, to compensate for a more powerful and pervasive, if sometimes less obviously conscious, double standard applied by white society.

Grier recalls reading about the response of some blacks after Brawley's story was exposed to be a fraud. They continued to believe her, and when pressed by a reporter, responded, "If it didn't happen, it could have happened."

Grier himself has a similar take on the Simpson case.

"If they didn't frame him, it's because nobody thought about framing him, everybody was busy framing somebody else," he says. "White people see the L.A. police department and prosecutor's office as a relatively neutral organ of the state. I don't know any black in the area who sees them that way."

Grier tells the story of his son, actor David Alan Grier, a regular on the Fox comedy show *In Living Color*, who was filming a scene in Los Angeles, dressed as a yuppie getting into a $100,000 Maserati. Oblivious to the whirring cameras, Grier says, "The cops drive up and grab my son and say, 'Whose car is this?' "

"I don't think a white person's ever had an experience like that," says Grier. As a black person, he says, "Your view of the world is truly different."

Harvard University psychiatrist Alvin Poussaint agrees.

"We still don't feel like we're full members of society," says Poussaint. "We still have so many examples of mistreatment that operate in institutionalized ways, whether it's the studies of blacks and whites going to buy a car and the whites getting it cheaper, or discrimination in housing, or trying to hail a taxicab."

The sense of psychic assault is so pervasive, says Poussaint, that even when he hears a thoroughly bizarre story about some conspiracy against the black community, "I just can't dismiss it that quickly."

In her book Turner analyzes such seemingly paranoid rumors as those claiming that national fried chicken franchises are owned by the Ku Klux Klan and add a secret ingredient to sterilize black men, and the more generalized fears of a conspiracy to destroy the black community with crack or AIDS.

As absurd as they sound, Turner says the rumors serve a purpose: They enunciate generalized black grievances—and mobilize resistance—against companies that exploit the black community or peddle destructive products, or against a government that too little values black life.

While it is hard to know how widely people believe the rumors Turner writes about, in a recent national survey of the black community, University of Chicago political scientist Michael Dawson found that 25 percent of blacks agree that AIDS is an anti-black conspiracy. (In that and other surveys, Dawson found a racial gap of 20 percent to 30 percent on a wide variety of political issues, even those with little ostensible connection to race.)

Turner is cautious about polling. Her experience in interviewing people is that someone who says they "believe" a particular rumor, often means that they find it "plausible."

And, for example, the AIDS rumor resonates with a people familiar with the Tuskegee experiment, in which for 40 years, until the early 1970s, the Public Health Service observed black men die of syphilis, rather than treat them, without letting them know what it was the health service was doing.

And, of course, it was something more than black paranoia that led Denny's, the nation's largest full-service family restaurant chain, to recently pay $54 million (while acknowledging nothing) to settle lawsuits by black customers who complained of systematically rude and inferior service.

Turner thinks it is more likely that the racism charged against Denny's is commonplace, and that Denny's served as a lightning rod for black resentment because it is, like many of the rumor targets in her book, the biggest.

It was Turner, in her book, who brought together the scholarship indicating that blacks and whites viewed each other as cannibals at the onset of the relationship.

It was, she found, a rumor that they would soon be eaten that precipitated the 1839 slave mutiny aboard the Spanish slaver, *Amistad*. The leader of the mutiny, Cinque, was quoted as saying, "We may as well die in trying to be free as to be killed and eaten."

Turner says it is only in the past 20 years that the myth of widespread cannibalism in Africa has come undone.

In this context, it is interesting that NAACP Executive Director Benjamin Chavis decried the intense focus on the Simpson case as racist because there had not been parallel obsession with Jeffrey Dahmer.

To whites, this may have seemed a non sequitur. After all, Dahmer had never been a hero to anyone.

But to blacks it may have had subconscious echoes back to the days of Cinque, and the need yet today to place the interplay of evil and race in its proper perspective. Dahmer, after all, made his reputation by murdering and then eating young men of color.

Ultimately, Turner believes, America will continue to have separate black and white realities until blacks can be "shown evidence that all contemporary white leaders are not in fact out to destroy them, and whites . . . accept that their ancestors treated the ancestors of black Americans so harshly that the present generation still bears the scars."

Birmingham News, July 24, 1994, pp. 1C, 4C.

MULTIRACIALISM

The following article, by William Singleton III, shows how dubious and inadequate racial categories are. The census for the year 2000 may well reflect the increasingly complicated racial makeup of the United States, but it will be out of date when it appears, because new racial categories appear all the time. What Wright touches on in *Black Boy*, the porousness of the boundary line between "black" and "white," is becoming totally undeniable as people from around the world immigrate to America and as prejudices against "interracial" marriages break down. It is becoming harder to deny the humanity of everyone, regardless of racial affiliation. Tiger Woods is a case in point: This extremely popular golf pro has commented that his multiracial identity does not fit on any racial grid.

FROM WILLIAM C. SINGLETON III, "WHITE? BLACK? MULTI? BI?"
(1996)

Nine-year-old Ashleigh Miller looks white and her mother, Loretta Edwards, is white. But when it comes time to check boxes as to Ashleigh's racial identity, her mother prefers not to choose "white."

Ms. Edwards prefers not to choose "black," either, even though Ashleigh's father is black, Ms. Edwards said.

"My daughter gets very offended when someone calls her white or black, because she's neither one," Ms. Edwards said.

Ms. Edwards refused to finish filling out the papers to enroll her daughter in the Mobile County [Florida] school system because Ashleigh had to choose a race.

The issue of racial identification has become a sensitive one, particularly since the number of people who consider themselves "multiracial" or "biracial" is growing.

In 1970, there were fewer than 500,000 children of interracial couples, according to the U.S. Bureau of the Census. By 1990, that figure was slightly under 2 million. The figures include children of interracial unions other than from black and white relationships, although much of the attention is given to that segment.

Many people of mixed parentage or mixed relationships resent having to select for themselves or their children either "white" or "black" on forms asking their racial identities.

The federal government is studying whether to include a "multiracial" or "biracial" category on the census in the year 2000.

Also Ms. Edwards forced the issue by suing the state of Florida last year because it made her child choose either "white" or "black" to register for school in West Palm Beach. Her daughter eventually chose "white," Ms. Edwards said. "But if her father was there she would have chosen black," she added.

The suit against the Florida school system was switched to federal courts, she said.

When she went to register her daughter in the Mobile County school system two weeks ago, Ms. Edwards entered "mixed" as her race. However, an official working in the registrar's office returned the form, saying the computer would not take it.

"She said, 'Well, we'll just put the race that you are in the computer,' " Ms. Edwards said. Ms. Edwards said she responded, "So what you're telling me is that without my consent, without my permission and without me even knowing you're going to give her a race. She said, 'Pretty much.' "

Tom Salter, a spokesman for the Mobile school system, said no one knows how many of the 65,000 students might be multiracial because the issue has not been raised until now.

"I don't believe there is some sort of evil plan behind this," he said. "I think it's just a question of the forms catching up with reality."

Since 1977, the Census Bureau has used four categories in classifying ethnicity: black, white, American Indian and Alaska native, and Asian and Pacific Islander. However, an "other" category and one for those of "Hispanic" or "Spanish" origin were added to the 1990 census.

The federal Office of Management and Budget has been evaluating federal guidelines—Federal Statistical Directive 15—on race and ethnic standards since 1993. Since then, OMB has held four public hearings on those guidelines, and in August 1995 it released a review based on comments from those hearings.

"During that review there were a number of issues that came up as it relates to Directive 15," said Claudette Bennett, statistical demographer for the Census Bureau in suburban Maryland. "The directive was criticized for not keeping pace with the changing racial and ethnic diversity of the U.S. population."

Suggestions from the hearing included adding a "multiracial" category and one embracing "Arab-American and Middle Eastern Americans," she said.

The bureau is conducting additional surveys and tests on the issue, including the Race and Ethnic Targeted Test. That test will be mailed to 90,000 households nationwide and will include a "multiracial" or "biracial" classification and a "check more than one category."

The test results will help OMB formulate its decision, which is expected sometime next year, Ms. Bennett said.

Efforts to create another racial category are not without controversy. Many civil rights groups such as the National Urban League, the National Association for the Advancement of Colored People and Lawyers' Committee for Civil Rights Under Law oppose a new multiracial category.

Such groups say a new category would water down the black vote as well as dilute benefits racial minorities receive under law.

According to the Lawyers' Committee for Civil Rights Under Law, amendments to the Constitution and civil rights laws acknowledge "skin color as a protected classification from discrimination."

"The current classifications have been indispensable in enforcing civil rights laws for historically disadvantaged people," said Barbara R. Arnwine, executive director of the Washington-based group. "Since the early 1980s, demographic data compiled under existing standards have been used to ensure that the electoral power of blacks and other protected classes is not unlawfully diluted when districts are created," Ms. Arnwine said.

"Likewise, overcoming the long history of discrimination in employment, lending, housing and education requires that demographic data be kept on racial and ethnic groups who have historically been subject to discrimination of one kind or another."

George Munchus, director of the Center for Research on Human Rights in Birmingham, said another racial classification probably would be cumbersome. Although he respects a person's right to be classified however he or she wishes, Munchus said, "it only adds confusion to the whole issue of how we as people define ourselves."

Besides, in some sense, all people are biracial or multiracial, he said.

But some Birmingham interracial couples or parents who have mixed children say they should have an option other than those currently provided.

"I've told my children to claim all of who they are," said Smith Williams, who is black and whose wife is white. "I just encourage them to check black and white, because that's what they are."

That has not presented much of a problem so far, Williams said. But many government agencies and public schools will not allow an applicant to select both categories.

Williams, who has a 12-year-old daughter and a 14-year-old son, says he favors a category that "does not limit people to black or white."

Another Birmingham woman, who did not want to be identified, said her 13-year-old son chooses "Hispanic" when he is asked his race, even though his mother is black and his father is of Irish descent.

"He has taken the term Hispanic because it implies interracial," she said.

One of the groups actively pushing for a "multiracial" category is Project RACE (Reclassify All Children Equally), based in Roswell, Ga.

Susan Graham, Project RACE executive director, said the category "other" and a fill-in-the-blank approach are not a substitute for a multiracial category.

"What happens when you say fill in your race or a combination of races, people will put things like Russian, Texan, alien," said Ms. Graham, who is white and married to a black man.

Censuses before 1920 attempted to reflect racial distinction and color lines. For example, the color of slaves in many states was recorded as either "black" or "mulatto," a term used to describe the offspring of a white and any person of color, whether an Indian or one of African descent.

However, after 1920, "the Census Bureau estimated that three-quarters of all African-Americans in the United States were racially mixed, and, therefore, no longer needed to be broken down into subracial distinctions," according to a committee report by the Lawyers' Committee for Civil Rights Under the Law called "New Racial Classifications in 2000 Census." "Subsequently, anyone with African ancestry at all would be counted simply as black," the report stated.

That led to the myth that one drop of black blood makes a person black. Many states adopted legal policies around that belief.

But Ms. Graham said such notions are antiquated. "I've had legislators call me to say, 'You can do this because of the one-drop law.' And I'll say, 'Show me the one-drop law. There isn't any such law.' "

She also takes exception to racial inquiries that ask mixed-race people to select the race they are most associated with. "To say 'Which race do you affiliate with most?' defeats the purpose of a multiracial classification," she said. "The [biracial] community knows we need a multiracial category."

Project RACE, Ms. Graham said, understands the concerns of civil rights leaders who believe a new multiracial designation will dilute black voting power.

But a 1995 survey by the Bureau of Labor Statistics, she said, indicates otherwise. According to that survey, slightly more than 1.5 percent of the respondents considered themselves "multiracial." The survey also seemed to indicate that when the multiracial category was available, there was no significant decline in the number of people identifying themselves as white, black or Asian.

Indians were the only group that showed any significant decline, according to the survey.

Ms. Edwards said the federal government needs to provide a broader designation because many states use the racial categories devised by OMB.

Both Ms. Edwards and Ms. Graham said an even more pressing reason for a broader racial designation is that the lives of mixed-race children depend on it.

It is difficult to get a bone marrow match for a multiracial child, particularly since statistics are not kept on them, Ms. Edwards said.

"They can't get bone marrow, they can't get blood donors, they can't get anything because they [the medical and governmental establishments] don't even acknowledge that they exist," Ms. Edwards said.

A Multiracial Solidarity March is scheduled July 20 in Washington, and Project RACE is sponsoring a bone marrow drive to raise awareness of this issue, Ms. Graham said. "Our children have been rendered invisible in the health care system in this country," she said.

Meanwhile, Ms. Edwards said, with a lawsuit pending she probably will enroll Ashleigh in school and let her daughter choose either "white" or "black" on school forms.

"But I wish there was another choice," Ms. Edwards said.

Birmingham News, July 13, 1996, p. 1C.

STUDY QUESTIONS

1. After reading *Black Boy* and the documents in this chapter, do you think America is obsessed with race? If so, why?

2. In your opinion, is racism increasing, declining, or staying the same?

3. Are Tillinghast's preconceptions about Africans based on racist reversals of his own values? For instance, whites are sexually responsible, whereas Africans are the opposite?

4. How widespread are Tillinghast's beliefs now?

5. Is Tillinghast looking at the real Africa or some racist fantasy of Africa?

6. Why does Tillinghast not recognize the horrible consequences of his kind of thinking?

7. Why does Tillinghast think that Africans will never be able to compete with whites?

8. What does Tillinghast imply is the reason whites like to see Africa as "backward"?

9. Why does Baker not seem to grasp the enormity of the crime of lynching? Why does he not see it from Wright's point of view?

10. What does Baker think will stop lynching?

11. Why is Sumner so complacent about pre–Civil War race relations?

12. What does Sumner mean by "southern society"?

13. Jean Finot condemns racial prejudice, yet sees black people as childlike. Why?

14. Finot's attitude toward African Americans is clearly less biased than Tillinghast's, yet his view is still less than accurate. How can you tell?

15. Through what kind of lens does Alfred Holt Stone see black Americans?

16. Why is Stone so complacent about what he regards as the inferiority of black people? What might have changed his mind, or the minds of the white people in *Black Boy*, about blacks?

17. What does Stone imply is likely to be the outcome of racial conflict if blacks come to think they are equal to whites?

18. Why would Bilbo have made such outrageous statements before the United States Senate?

19. Is it surprising to you that Tilove says that the Africans on the slave ships thought the whites were going to eat them? Why or why not? What is the irony in Tilove's charge?

20. How close does Wright come to seeing whites as cannibals in *Black Boy*?

21. What would your attitude be toward someone who enslaved and sold you?

22. If the trends Singleton notes in his article persist, will racism disappear because everyone will be multiracial, or do you think some other category will replace race as a marker of social value?

23. Would Wright, if he were still alive, be surprised at Singleton's essay? Why or why not?

TOPICS FOR WRITTEN OR ORAL EXPLORATION

1. Write a paper in which you explain Wright's success in *Black Boy* in attacking the ludicrous notions about race expressed in some of the documents in this chapter.

2. Discuss Wright's concept of race in *Black Boy*. What is it based on?

3. How heavily invested are you, your family, and your friends in the concept of race? How would you account for this investment?

4. Do you know of any politicians today who use a more sophisticated version of Senator Bilbo's strategy to win votes? If so, who are they and what are their positions?

5. If race and racism ever cease to be issues in America, do you think *Black Boy* will then cease to be of interest?

6. Why are interracial dating and marriage still considered taboo by many Americans?

7. If differences are what define us, will different racial groups in America need to persist in their hostility toward each other in order to maintain their group identity?

8. Why is the notion of "superiority" too heavy a burden for any individual or group to carry?

9. Write a paper discussing what you see as current attitudes on racism as expressed by blacks and whites. Refer to recent high-profile court cases that polarized black and white America.

SUGGESTED READINGS

Aptheker, Herbert. *Antiracism in U.S. History*. Westport, Conn.: Greenwood Press, 1992.

Ashmore, Harry S. *Hearts and Minds: The Anatomy of Racism from Roosevelt to Reagan*. New York: McGraw-Hill, 1982.

Bell, Derrick A. *Faces at the Bottom of the Well*. New York: Basic Books, 1992.

Butterfield, Fox. *All God's Children: The Bosket Family and the American Tradition of Violence*. New York: Knopf, 1995.

Campbell, Christopher P. *Races, Myth and the News*. Thousand Oaks, Calif.: Sage Publications, 1995.

Cruse, Harold. *The Crisis of the Negro Intellectual*. New York: William Morrow, 1967.

Davis, F. James. *Who Is Black? One Nation's Definition*. University Park: Pennsylvania State University Press, 1991.

D'Souza, Dinesh. *The End of Racism*. New York: Free Press, 1995.

Ezekiel, Raphael S. *The Racist Mind*. New York: Viking, 1995.

Fanon, Frantz. *Black Skin, White Masks*. New York: Grove Press, 1967.

———. *The Wretched of the Earth*. New York: Grove Press, 1963.

Feagin, Joe R. *Living with Racism*. Boston: Beacon Press, 1994.

Fraizer, E. Franklin. *The Negro Family in the United States*. Chicago: University of Chicago Press, 1939.

Fredrickson, George M. *The Arrogance of Racism*. Middletown, Conn.: Wesleyan University Press, 1992.

Giovanni, Nikki. *Racism 101*. New York: William Morrow, 1994.

Gordon, Lewis R. *Bad Faith and Antiblack Racism*. Atlantic Highlands, N.J.: Humanities Press, 1995.

Gounard, Jean Français. *The Racial Problem in the Works of Richard Wright and James Baldwin*. Westport, Conn.: Greenwood Press, 1992.

Graham, Lawrence. *Member of the Club: Reflections on Life in a Racially Polarized World*. New York: HarperCollins, 1995.

Griffin, John Howard. *Black Like Me*. New York: New American Library, 1960.

Hacker, Andrew. *Two Nations: Black and White, Separate, Hostile, Unequal*. New York: Scribner's, 1992.

Herskovits, Melville J. *The Myth of the Negro Past*. Boston: Beacon Press, 1941.

hooks, bell. *Killing Rage: Ending Racism*. New York: Henry Holt, 1995.

Jackson, Jesse. *Legal Lynching: Racism, Injustice, and the Death Penalty*. New York: Marlowe, 1996.

Kleg, Milton. *Hate, Prejudice and Racism*. Albany: State University of New York Press, 1993.

Kovel, Joel. *White Racism: A Psychohistory*. New York: Columbia University Press, 1984.

Loury, Glenn C. *One by One from the Inside Out: Essays and Reviews on Race and Responsibility in America*. New York: Free Press, 1995.

McClorey, Robert. *Racism in America: From Milk and Honey to Ham and Eggs*. Chicago: Fides/Claretron, 1981.

Powell, Thomas F. *The Persistence of Racism in America*. Lanham, Md.: Littlefield, Adams, 1993.

Robinson, James L. *Racism or Attitude? The Ongoing Struggle for Black Liberation and Self-Esteem*. New York: Insight Books, 1995.

Ropers, Richard H. *American Prejudice: With Liberty and Justice for Some*. New York: Insight Books, 1995.

Sanders, Ronald. *Lost Tribes and Promised Lands: The Origins of American Racism*. Boston: Little, Brown, 1978.

Shapiro, Herbert. *White Violence and Black Response: From Reconstruction to Montgomery*. Amherst: University of Massachusetts Press, 1988.

Shipman, Pat. *The Evolution of Racism*. New York: Simon and Schuster, 1994.

Small, Stephen. *Racialised Barriers*. New York: Routledge, 1994.

Sniderman, Paul M. *The Scar of Race*. Cambridge, Mass.: Belknap Press, 1993.

Steele, Shelby. *The Content of Our Character*. New York: St. Martin's Press, 1990.

Vaughn, Alden T. *Roots of American Racism*. New York: Oxford University Press, 1995.

West, Cornel. *Race Matters*. New York: Vintage Books, 1993.

Williams, Vernon J. *Rethinking Race: Franz Boas and His Contemporaries*. Livingston: University Press of Kentucky, 1996.

Index

About the Author

ROBERT FELGAR is Professor of English and Head of the English Department at Jacksonville State University in Jacksonville, Alabama. He is author of *Richard Wright* (1980), as well as numerous articles on black literature, Robert Browning, and Mississippi writers. He directed two Summer Seminars for School Teachers on "The Achievement of Richard Wright" under the sponsorship of the National Endowment for the Humanities. He is currently writing articles on Wright's novel *Native Son*.